An Insider's View of Rocky Flats:
Urban Myths Debunked

by

Farrel D. Hobbs

An Insider's View of Rocky Flats:
Urban Myths Debunked

© Copyright 2010
by Farrel D. Hobbs

Cover design by K. M. Motyl Associates.

Cover photographs courtesy of the U.S. Department of Energy.

ISBN-13:978-1460911471
ISBN-10:1460911474

Please visit www.RockyFlatsFacts.com for current discussions and
additional information regarding the Rocky Flats story.

Acknowledgements

I decided to write and publish this book because the raid in 1989 and the following investigation created distrust and concern among our neighbors and probably even among some of my coworkers. Pride began to be replaced by discomfort in mentioning where we worked. I hope that discomfort can be put aside after reading this book. It was written based on my first-hand experiences during the raid and investigations and extensive research of public documents. I don't claim to be a "Rocky Flats expert," because it is certain every individual who worked there could add other insights and stories. I will assure you the massive investigation of Rocky Flats proved we were working diligently to carefully manage radioactive and hazardous materials and that these were processed safely and in compliance with the laws of the land.

This book would not have been written without the remarkable accomplishments and legacy of the people who worked at Rocky Flats and my first acknowledgment goes to them. I worked directly with people in research and development, production, environmental, and procurement. I collaborated with others in health and safety, engineering, security, personnel, and the maintenance and support organizations that provided all the services that allowed the Plant to operate like an effective small city. Rocky Flats was a proud place, and it deserved to be proud of the significant contributions it made to the nation's security while being a good neighbor. There were even more amazing accomplishments in the closure of the site after the nation decided it was no longer needed.

I also want to acknowledge the expertise and insights provided by Sally Kribs and Barb Warden. Their editing and suggestions converted a very rough effort into a book that has generated mostly complementary comments. I have served as my own final editor, so any interesting uses of the English language that remain are undoubtedly my contribution. I also want to recognize Keith Motyl's efforts to create both www.RockyFlatsFacts.com, and this version of the book. I encourage readers to check that site and its blog postings for current discussions. The online version of the book has created, for example, significant discussion about health risks from plutonium.

Contents

Prologue

In the late 1960s Americans were dealing with a full-scale conventional war in Vietnam, and the surreal possibility of nuclear war from some accidental or intentional escalation of the Cold War. The United States and the Soviet Union both had sufficient warheads and delivery systems to make the Mutually Assured Destruction (MAD) policy a reality, but were continually improving and adding to their massive arsenals. Britain, China, and France and perhaps Israel also had nuclear weapons.

Spies and counterspies were active anywhere there was nuclear weapons research or construction. The Soviets had begun building their arsenal using information stolen from the Manhattan Project through a spy ring code named "Enormoz" to assemble and detonate their first atomic bomb in 1949 at a place called Semipalatinsk. Other countries were impressed by the efficiency of that approach.

The Cold War, the Vietnam War, and increasingly angry protests dominated news reports. Traditional ideas about patriotism were being challenged as young people became increasingly skeptical about the establishment.

That's a short version of what was happening in the world when I completed my U.S. Army enlistment and went to work at Rocky Flats in early 1969. I was given a tour of a production area about three months after starting the new job when my security clearance was granted. The memory of being handed a stainless steel case containing plutonium and feeling the surprising weight and heat generated by the radioactive energy remains quite clear after four decades.

Chapter 1

Rocky Flats Interview

or

Secrecy and Communicating Don't Mix

I don't recall hearing the name "Rocky Flats" until my Army enlistment was nearly complete. I had been called for military service as the Vietnam War had demanded more replacement soldiers. There had been nearly a year of infantry training before I was commissioned under oath to defend the country and uphold its laws. A colonel in the Army section of the North American Air Defense Command (NORAD) had me assigned to work with him because of my military training and my degree in chemistry. The Cold War mission of the branch of NORAD where I worked was to provide major metropolitan areas protection with surface to air missiles. Many of the missiles had nuclear warheads. I performed my assigned share of the watch over the nuclear arsenal at missile bases around the country, my Colorado Springs office, and twice inside Cheyenne Mountain.

My superior officers wanted me to reenlist, but I began searching for a civilian job. I went on a few interviews and was offered a few jobs. The job market was excellent because many thousands of potential applicants were overseas. The master sergeant I worked with told me he had seen a help wanted ad for a chemist at a place near Boulder, Colorado. I found the ad, but it didn't offer much information about the position, indicating only that there was an opening for a chemist. The possibility of finding employment in Colorado was enough of a lure for me to place a call with an inquiry. I learned nothing about the position, but was told the address where I could send my resume. A few days later I was invited for an interview. The time of the interview and driving directions were the only details I was given.

I made the drive from Colorado Springs to Highway 93 between Golden and Boulder and found the west access road that had been described as the way to the Rocky Flats Plant. I located the parking lot and building where I had been told to report and was greeted by an armed guard. He looked me over, asked for identification, checked a list, and directed me into a tiny, windowless office.

My interviewer came in the door at precisely the appointed time, and studied me with what I can only describe as an intense glare. We exchanged names and a perfunctory handshake, and sat down. The interviewer began looking though a file. He reminded me of a no-nonsense military officer.

"Have you ever done any high vacuum research?"

That's how the interview began. No gratitude was expressed for my interest in a job. There were no questions about family or interests. The interviewer simply began asking questions about my experience. He quickly determined that I had no experience with vacuum systems, welding, metallurgy, or cryogenics. The only positive answer I could give was to a question as to whether I was assigned to NORAD. But then I was asked what I knew about the warheads, and I had to say I couldn't talk about that. That seemed to end the interview. I was asked if I had any questions, I inquired what the job would be, and the interviewer told me he couldn't tell me that. I figured that was an excellent clue the interview had gone just as poorly as I feared. I certainly didn't know that I was going to get a job offer because I refused to respond to a question that could have led to classified information.

My wife was eager to hear about the interview, and disappointed when I told her the interview had gone poorly. We were quite surprised when the Rocky Flats personnel department called two days later to offer me a job. My wife and I were curious about taking a job that hadn't yet been described to me, but we decided the interviewer must have believed I could do the work. We decided I should accept the job, because we wanted to stay in Colorado.

My wife, baby son, and I were moving into an apartment in Broomfield, Colorado in about a month. It wasn't long before I began my first drive to Rocky Flats as an employee, nervous and wondering what I would be asked to do.

Chapter 2

First Months at Rocky Flats
or
Some Day I'll Learn Why I Was Hired

I began the drive towards the Colorado foothills reflecting on how it felt to be going to a civilian job dressed in civilian clothes. I preferred to think about that rather than focus on the anticipation of actually starting the job. I was curious and nervous about what my job would be. Looking back, I wonder how nervous I would have been if I had known what would be happening in the next few months.

I arrived at the administration building for the second time, and soon realized I wouldn't learn anything about my job. No one from my new organization was there to meet me. A guard handed me a red badge and told me that indicated I didn't have a security clearance. That was somewhat baffling, since I had a clearance in the Army. I was sent to the personnel department to fill out paperwork, and was told the job required an Atomic Energy Commission (AEC) "Q" clearance, and that a full background check would be performed by federal agents. I wondered whether having a brother-in-law who advocated socialism could prevent me from being granted a Q clearance. Word reached me later that agents were in my hometown in Kansas interviewing people about my background and character.

The word filtering back to me about the clearance investigation was certainly more interesting than my initial job at Rocky Flats. I was sent to the procurement department, shown to a sparse office, and handed a stack of purchase requisitions. My assignment was to check that dollar amounts had been added accurately. I quickly learned the people around me wouldn't discuss the site or its mission. I did observe that many of the requisitions were for purchase of a variety of metals. It was also apparent someone else had checked the accuracy of the math on the requisitions. I never found an error.

It was a slow two months of trying to remain enthusiastic or at least trying to not look completely disinterested in purchase requisitions. My concerns about whether I would be able to handle the new job certainly were wasted on the initial assignment.

I was relieved when I received a call that my security clearance had been granted. One of the people in my organization came to take me through the badging process and to show me to my new workplace. I was soon wearing my green-bordered picture badge that served as visible evidence of a Q security clearance. We walked to another building and I

3

was issued a radiation-measuring device called a dosimeter. It confirmed I would be working with radioactive materials, which was something I had speculated about while contemplating the interview question about warheads. My green Q clearance security badge slid into the dosimeter holder, and that was clipped to my collar. Then we began our walk to the security areas. We walked through several security stations where I was told to hand the guards my new badge for confirmation that my face matched the picture. The guards seemed universally disinterested in my new experience. My guide was friendly and talkative, which was a welcome distraction. The proliferation of fences topped with rolls of razor wire, the non-descript gray concrete buildings, and the armed guards certainly all portrayed something much less friendly.

We made our way to Building 779, which fit in nicely with the other concrete buildings we passed. I was led to an office and desk on the second floor of the building, which was behind two sets of double doors. This arrangement was described as an air lock, and I was instructed to let the first doors close completely before pushing through the second set to the hallway beyond.

I was led around for introductions, and when I returned to my office, one of the people from my new work group was waiting for me.

"Want to see what we do?"

"Sure."

"Let's get you dressed out."

I was assigned a locker and key. I put my civilian clothes in the locker and changed into white underwear, coveralls, and some safety shoes. A person they called a "monitor" gave me a half-mask respirator and instructed me how to put it on, adjust it, and seal it. A simple test was performed to determine whether the respirator fit me properly. I was led down a hallway, told to put shoe covers that were called "booties," and we walked down a long hallway to another airlock.

We walked into a place like nothing I had ever seen or imagined. I'm trying to think how to describe the area, and it won't be easy to do it justice. We were in a large room with long lines of stainless steel enclosures raised to about waist high by metal legs above a cement floor. There were several people, and they were all dressed in white coveralls. Some were reaching into the enclosures through gloves attached to the metal walls. They were looking through windows at whatever they were doing. I was told the enclosures were called "glove boxes." The lines of glove boxes seemed to be endless as we walked through the Building 776/777 production area.

We came to a small cart holding two metal objects. My guide put on cotton gloves and instructed me to do the same. He then carefully picked up one of the shiny metal objects off the cart.

"I'm going to hand it to you and put my hands under yours as you hold it. Don't drop it, especially not before I get my hands under yours. Ready?"

"Yes."

I was handed the object and realized several people were watching, but all of my attention was instantly refocused on the object in my hands.

"Know what that is?"

"No."

"That's an atomic bomb."

Time moved very slowly for the next few moments, and I could feel my anxiety growing. My throat felt tight, and my voice sounded weak when I said, "It's heavy for its size."

"Plutonium is very heavy."

"Is this plutonium?"

"The plutonium is sealed inside steel."

"It's warm. Has it been in an oven?"

"No, it's always warm. There's lots of radioactive energy in plutonium and that keeps it warm."

We stood silent for a while before I asked, "Why are you holding your hands under mine?"

"Because someone dropped one once. They panicked when they heard what it was and jerked their hands back."

Chapter 3

The Mother's Day Fire

or

Tickling the Dragon's Tail

Learning what was made at Rocky Flats surprised me, but it didn't deter or frighten me. My reaction was more amazement that I had somehow found my way to the place where the plutonium parts in the missiles at NORAD had originated. I would learn that what I had held was not an atomic bomb, but instead was a plutonium component that would eventually be assembled into an atomic bomb at another location. That was just the beginning of what I learned. My first full week as a Q-cleared Rocky Flats employee was filled with a barrage of new information. I learned I had been correct in being nervous about the complexity of what I was expected to do. The work was going to be technically challenging. Much of the information and training emphasized safety, including detailed and strict requirements about working with and around radioactive materials. The need to keep it enclosed and myself and others protected was the focus. There were constant reminders that I was going to be working with dangerous materials. I knew of the very real threat posed by the Soviet nuclear arsenal, so I believed any risks were justified by the need for maintaining America's arsenal. I had no misgivings about the Rocky Flats mission; I believed the country needed what we were doing.

My wife quickly surmised that I wouldn't be talking about my job. She noticed I was wearing a green badge instead of the red one, and I told her my security clearance had been granted. That's about all I could tell her, or that I felt I could say. We found a way not to talk specifics about my assignment during my nearly two years at NORAD. We had plenty of practice with her not asking questions I couldn't answer.

Interactions with other workers in the research and development group were tense. The bosses advocated and encouraged a very competitive environment, and most of the people were sizing me up as to what kind of threat I might be to the existing pecking order. Not everyone participated in the competition. There were three co-workers who openly welcomed me and taught me what to expect, what to do, and who to trust. I continue to have great respect for those people. I learned quickly that I wasn't alone in believing in the Rocky Flats mission. The people I worked with often expressed pride about the work we were doing. Patriotic was the appropriate word to describe the Rocky Flats workforce in 1969.

May 11, 1969 was a memorable day. It was the first Mother's Day for my wife and our infant son. I don't recall what gift my son and I bought her to mark the occasion, but I do remember it was a special day. Little did we know that a few miles away from the celebration in our apartment that a fire was moving through glove box lines in Building 776/777. These were the same glove boxes I had seen for the first time a week earlier. The fire had burned off the gloves, melted and burned the windows, warped the steel structures, and converted the plutonium metal parts into piles of plutonium oxide.

I cannot imagine how frightening the fire must have been to the small weekend crew and firefighters who combated the fire. I commend plant management for their foresight in having firefighters available 24 hours a day. I give even more credit to firefighters for their courage. When they arrived the fire was moving through interconnected glove box lines, consuming everything that would burn. An AEC report describes what the firefighters faced and what they did:

> *Although the fire department responded quickly, the dense smoke, crowded conditions, and presence of large quantities of combustible shielding material made the fire very difficult to fight and extinguish. Because of the concern about the possibility of a nuclear criticality accident (a chain reaction), the standard firefighting procedures then in effect for Building 776/777 did not specify the use of water, except as a last resort. For this reason, there was no automatic sprinkler system in this area of the building. The first attack on the fire was made with CO2 and was ineffective. Less than ten minutes after the fire alarm was received, the fire captain initiated the use of water. Thereafter, water was used almost exclusively in the firefighting activities.* (AEC, December 1969, page 2).

The fire was so large it must have been obvious that the only way to fight it was with water, despite the risk of a criticality. A criticality occurs when the nuclear reaction becomes self-sustaining, and adding water can increase the risk of a criticality. Scientists who experimented to determine the amount of radioactive material necessary to create a criticality called the experimentation "tickling the dragon's tail." Imagine how careful you would be if you tickled a dragon's tail and it gives you a rudimentary understanding of how important it is to avoid an accidental criticality.

The firefighters entering the production area on May 11, 1969 could choose to use water to put the fire out, or they could choose to have the building burn down. A report prepared for the State of Colorado gives one answer as to why the decision was made to use water. The fire

7

captain arriving on the scene had been involved in a significant fire in Building 771 in 1957, and water had been used then. He directed his three firefighters to use water based on that previous experience. (Radiological Assessments Corporation, August 1999, page I)

The firefighters deployed the fire hoses and were able to bring the fire under control. They were wearing supplied air packs, but there was no time to decontaminate when the air in their tanks began to run out. They ran outside the west side of the building, threw off the nearly empty rigs, inhaled and swallowed some of the plutonium that was on their faces, put on a new rig, positioned the mask over their face, which was now contaminated with plutonium, and ran inside to rejoin the firefight. There was no criticality, because none of the firefighters or anyone else in the area suffered the horrific radiation burns that would have caused. I consider that these people performed heroically in a very frightening situation. They put their workplace and the communities around it above their own safety.

The majority of Rocky Flats workers had no knowledge of the fire until we began to report to work the next day, the beginning of my second week as a Q-cleared worker. I joined the crowd of workers passing through the security stations just like I did the week before. But unlike the previous week there were people at the entrance to Building 750 directing us to the cafeteria. There was a steady, low buzz of quiet conversations as many people asked each other what was going on, and none of us knew. We could only guess, but the conversations focused on speculating how bad things were.

Someone gave a very short briefing to a very quiet crowd. We were told a major fire had damaged the glove box lines in Building 776/777, and that we were to talk to no one outside of work about it. One of the research managers then gathered those of us assigned to Building 779 and took us to a conference room. We were told what was later included in the unclassified report about the fire. The capability to produce and assemble plutonium pits for War Reserve weapons would be lost for several months. All research plans were on hold until the burned area could be decontaminated and rebuilt. It was explained that the fire cleanup, decontamination, and rebuilding of the production lines was the number one national defense priority. There was a call for volunteers to enter the area and begin the work. One of the three people who had welcomed me during my first week volunteered, and I also held up my hand.

Chapter 4

Plutonium Decontamination After a Fire

or

My Assignment as a Human Q-Tip

Shortly after volunteering to work in the fire area, I was in a locker room as part of a crew of ten people. We were instructed to dress out in a set of coveralls, tape them at the wrists and ankles, put on another set, and repeat the taping process. Most of the coveralls were made for people whose arms and legs weren't as long as mine, so there was difficulty in taping the sleeves and legs. Someone told me to run the yellow tape, the tape used everywhere at Rocky Flats for contaminated work, down my wrists and ankles to compensate for the coveralls being a couple of inches too short.

We also put on multiple layers of surgeon's gloves after taping the first layer to the wrists of the coveralls (or in my case, the tape on my wrists). I seemed to struggle more than the others in taping the gloves without getting the latex fingers stuck to the tape.

We completed our outfits with skullcaps, safety shoes, double layers of booties over the shoes, safety glasses, and half-mask respirators. The transition to additional protection provided by full-face respirators didn't come until later. I was the last person to finish dressing out, but no one seemed to be in a rush.

We were led into the fire area, and it was a remarkable scene of destruction. The metal shells of the rows of glove boxes were intact, but most of the windows and gloves had been breached and burned. There were charred, melted, and distorted remnants of glove cuffs and windows and piles of ash as testimonials to the heat and destruction of the fire.

My assignment was to get on top of the metal skeleton of the boxes and begin construction of plastic dividers attached with yellow tape to the maze of pipes along the ceiling. The plan was to segregate the area into plastic rooms to facilitate the beginning of cleanup and decontamination.

Working conditions were miserable. I hadn't noticed during my tour of the area before the fire that the glove boxes had windows in the tops just as there were on the sides. All the windows were made of various specialty plastics, and all had been mostly melted or burned out. I had to walk on the metal sides that remained, one foot on each side of the missing windows. I could see the bottoms of the boxes were covered with a variety of ash over the different tools and machines. Occasionally there would be a pile of the ugly greenish gray ash I recognized from my week of training as plutonium oxide. That's where a plutonium part had been before the fire burned it from metal to oxide.

The massive contamination of the area wasn't what made the work miserable. The heat caused the misery. All ventilation had been shut down, and the temperature near the ceiling was well over 100 degrees. Sweat quickly soaked through all my clothing. I would learn the sweat-soaked coveralls were an excellent barrier to contamination from plutonium oxide, which is virtually insoluble in water. The outer clothing was quickly smeared and streaked with highly radioactive ash. Everything I touched while taping the plastic was covered with smut that would have caused a radiation detection meter to register off the scale, which was called "infinity" levels of contamination. My outer clothing was quickly at infinity. I've told many people that my first job after getting a Q clearance was serving as a human Q-tip.

I don't know how it happened, but I became separated from the rest of the work crew about two hours after we made our entry. I know I didn't cover much distance from where I initially began working on top of the boxes, but I was surprised when I looked around and saw that I was alone. I waited and watched for a short time, but began to feel concerned. Sweat had began to accumulate in the bottom of the half-mask respirator where the rubber formed a seal below my mouth, and I was literally gurgling unless I tipped my head back slightly to keep the layer of sweat below my lips. A growing sense of claustrophobia began to creep in, and I had to concentrate on breathing slow and deep to overcome the fear that was making me want to rip off the respirator.

Dehydration was beginning to be a problem. I guessed that I had lost maybe ten to fifteen pounds in water weight based on my experience with rigorous exercise during military physical training. I reasoned that I couldn't continue any productive work, since there was no one on the floor to hand up new pieces of plastic. I finally climbed down the ladder beside the box and began tracing my way back to where we had entered. I encountered a group of people dressed in garb identical to mine, only much cleaner, walking into the area. One of them told me to go back.

"We have to work our full shift."

It was tough, but I made it. The discipline to mentally overcome physical stress learned in the military got me through. Finally the word came for us to exit.

We arrived at the exit and began stripping away layers of clothes until the last of the contamination was removed. I was relieved I was able to shed all the contamination, and my skin was clean. There would be other times when a decontamination shower would be required to remove the traces of plutonium oxide that made it through the clothing and onto the skin. I've heard stories about people who had their skin scrubbed with wire brushes and bleach. It never happened to me, and I never observed it or heard of it happening to anyone else until years later when the movie "*Silkwood*" portrayed that decontamination process at another facility. That doesn't mean it didn't happen, but it wasn't part of my experience. I do know I was pleased that no decontamination was needed at my first exit from the fire area. I wanted nothing more than to get out and find some drinking water.

The most interesting part of leaving the fire area for the first time was that the other workers in my crew were in the locker room dressing out for another entry. They had left me and I had worked a double shift. It hadn't registered with me when I found the crew coming toward me as I was attempting to leave. Everyone looks the same when dressed out with respirators, safety glasses, and skullcaps covering their features, so I hadn't realized these were different people. Startled looks were exchanged when my crew and I saw each other, but no one said anything, including me. That moment moved my status up to someone who wouldn't rat out coworkers. Taking a head count was adopted to assure everyone was together before we exited the area during the following days and weeks.

Chapter 5

Fire Flies in the Glove Box
or
A Sight Glove Box Workers Don't Like

My assignment to the decontamination effort lasted a few weeks before I was reassigned to watching over a crew of uncleared workers a few years younger than me who had been hired to do decontamination of an unclassified area. All of the members of the crew were young adult children of Rocky Flats workers. The area we were assigned to decontaminate was the second floor of Building 776, and we worked the evening shift. I've heard some people said in later years that the fire had burned through the second floor of the building and then through the roof. I walked all over the second floor of the building with the exception of inside the filter plenums, and the floor I walked on and the ceiling above me were intact and undamaged. I also heard rumors that the first set of filters used to treat contaminated air before release had been damaged from the heat. I recall looking through a port-sized window into the plenums, and couldn't see any damage, perhaps because the lighting was poor.

The official AEC accident report about the fire and its aftermath stated, "The fire did not breach the building roof, and only a small part of one exhaust filter system was ruptured. Consequently, most of the smoke and essentially all of the plutonium remained in the building." (AEC, August 1969, page 3) The Radiological Assessments Corporation was hired by Colorado to investigate the history of radiation releases at Rocky Flats in the 1990s. Their report concluded "Relatively little plutonium was released to the atmosphere during the fire because of (a) the captain's decision to use water to fight the fire, (b) the persistence of the firemen, who made repeated entries into the building, and (c) the exhaust systems containing multiple sets of nonflammable high-efficiency particulate air (HEPA) filters were damaged but remained intact." (Radiological Assessments Corporation, August 1999, page ii)

There was, however, no doubt that the second floor area where we worked was contaminated, although not nearly to the extent of the area on the first floor where the glove boxes had burned. Nevertheless, the area had to be decontaminated, and the young workers were a good bunch of people who worked hard at their jobs.

The work was low-tech and tedious: Wet a Kimwipe® with 409® cleaner, the cleaning solution of preference, and wipe down the surface. Toss the wipe to the floor and repeat the process a couple more times.

Then move to the next spot. We would take turns gathering the wipes from the floor and putting them into plastic bags for disposal as contaminated waste. The working conditions were uncomfortable with no ventilation to keep us from sweating through our layers of clothing, and the work was repetitious and boring. I worked beside the crew with my own box of wipes and container of cleaner, but my primary job was keeping the young crew from taking unsafe short cuts such as swinging to a new decontamination position on a pipe instead of moving a ladder. I occasionally had to intercede when some of the old hands among the regular work force chided the young workers.

I thought my assignment went well, although I never became acclimated to the evening shift. I often wished I were in better physical condition, because the work was very tiring. About four weeks into the work, my boss told me I had a new assignment.

"We need you to clean some old ingots."

"Okay."

"The ingots have been in the criticality lab for years, and there is a flash of stuff burning when the cans are opened in the glove boxes. Some describe it as a sort of suppressed flash, like when the old time photographers took a picture, but maybe not that bright. Others say it looks more like a hundred or a thousand fireflies being released into the box. Makes them nervous. Anything that burns is a bad thing right now."

The ingots had been taken out of glove boxes into heavy plastic bags. The bags were taped closed and put into large cans that were originally made to transport movie film. The plastic bag-encased ingots had been in storage for years, and were quite hot in both thermal and radiation terms. Direct contact between the ingots and the bags caused the plastic to discolor, become brittle, and disintegrate over the years of storage. The hydrogen and oxygen released from the disintegrating plastic reacted with the plutonium metal to form reaction products that were capable of burning spontaneously when exposed to air. The small particles of those reaction products would become suspended and ignite when the lid of the film can was removed. This created the "fire flies" that had startled the workers.

Another worker and I were to remove the flammable particles from the ingots in a glove box that had enough nitrogen added to keep oxygen below the level needed to sustain a fire. The object was to clean and repackage the ingots for delivery to the production people.

The process we followed after scrubbing the surface of the ingots clean with Scotch-brite® in the inerted glove box was to bag them out of the line and take them to a "downdraft table." This was an enclosure perhaps four times the area of a telephone booth. The "table" had a coarse wire mesh screen in the middle, and the downdraft was a rapid airflow pulled down though the screen by a remote vacuum-creating fan. Contaminated materials could be handled on or above the screen without releasing contamination in the breathing zone of the people working over the table. However, we wore respirators and the usual protective clothes, including several layers of latex gloves.

The plastic bag containing the ingot was put onto the wire mesh screen. The first person would cut the bag open and pick up the ingot. The second person would be ready with a large strip of aluminum foil. The foil was carefully wrapped around the ingot while the first worker removed the contaminated surgeon gloves, dropped them into the contaminated trash, and had the new pair of gloves checked by the third person, the radiation monitor. Another strip of aluminum foil was added following the confirmation that the gloves were free of contamination, and this process was repeated until the ingot was completely encased in "cold," or uncontaminated, foil. The packaged ingot could then be loaded into a new film can and put onto a cart for delivery to production.

Two bad things happened to me while working on the ingot-cleaning project. The first was a "little joke" based on the significant weight and thermal heat of the ingots. The monitor working with us pretended to be having trouble with the radiation detection instrument while I was holding the foil-wrapped ingot over the downdraft table. The weight of the ingot quickly made my muscles quiver. The heat began to be painful. But I was not to set the ingot down, or the entire process would be wasted, and we would have to start over. The senior technician who was working with me saw what was happening, understood this was a "little joke," and commanded the monitor to stop messing around (only in less polite language). The monitor cleared my partner to wrap the ingot into another layer of foil, which relieved me of the weight and heat. The monitor looked a bit sheepish when we finished and I removed the final sets of surgeon gloves from shaking hands. My palms looked sunburned.

A more serious incident happened later when we were loading a film can containing an ingot into the glove box line. My coworker placed the can down into the top-loading box with the ventilation flowing full force down into the box. The tips of his gloved fingers were trapped under the weight of the can. He pulled his hands free, which caused the can to suddenly drop the very short distance to the floor of the box. We didn't know the sudden drop of the can that short distance had caused a puff of plutonium contamination to be released into our breathing air until the alarm on the alpha radiation monitor sounded. We put on our respirators and waited for the help that arrived in minutes. The monitor found contamination on the left side of my face, including into my left nostril. The lung count at the medical facility detected radioactive contamination in my left lung.

My personal experience doesn't support the concept commonly stated that one small particle of plutonium is deadly. I haven't developed lung cancer in the more than forty years since the inhalation, and I was a heavy smoker for twenty or so of those years.

Chapter 6

The Hourly Strike
or
Criticize Safety To Get What You Want

The cleanup and decontamination of Building 776/777 progressed, but there were changes in and around Rocky Flats. An outside group became quite concerned when word of the fire began to leak to the public. The group collected samples of soil east of the plant, and found plutonium contamination. When confronted with this information, someone at the site responded that the recent fire hadn't caused the contamination. The 1957 fire in Building 771 caused some of it, and some came from wind-blown spread of contamination from the 903 pad storage area. The information didn't make anyone more comfortable. What fire in 1957 and what is the 903 pad storage area? A description of the 1957 fire, which breeched the filter plenums in Building 771, was provided. The other source of contamination was created when the AEC decided to store drums of plutonium-contaminated machining oil mixed with carbon tetrachloride on a dirt area known as the 903 pad. Dow Chemical, the operating contractor that managed Rocky Flats for the first few decades, had disagreed with the decision, and argued diligently and unsuccessfully to have the decision reversed. Dow was overruled, told that AEC owned the site, and that their job was to do what they were told by AEC. This apparently was one of the few times Dow listened to AEC, and they learned from the experience. The drums were stored outside and corroded. The oil leaked, and the wind began to distribute the plutonium.

The explanations that the contamination releases had been from these previous events and not the 1969 fire created understandable distrust. The site began a downward slide of negative publicity that never ended.

The controversy had little effect on me; I was able to leave thoughts of Rocky Flats at the exit gates each evening as I drove or rode with my carpool back to Broomfield. My wife, young son, and I settled into a comfortable life. My work as a decontamination worker, crew leader, and plutonium ingot cleaner ended, and I began the production support work I had been hired to do. My wife and I bought our first home in Northglenn, Colorado, and we moved in to wait for our daughter to be born. We were getting by on the pay and benefits from Rocky Flats, and life was good.

However, it wasn't long before there were stirrings of union contract trouble. Negotiations between the union that represented the bargaining unit employees and Dow Chemical, a company that wasn't a big fan of unions, weren't going well. The negotiations failed and a strike began.

16

The strikers picketing and blocking the plant entrance were in a celebratory mood the first morning of the strike. Salaried workers were prevented from entering the plant, and we lined up our cars along the sides of Highway 93 waiting for word of what we should do. A court order was issued within a couple of hours, and the picketers had to separate to allow us to drive into the plant. Most of the strikers were smiling and waving.

The plant managers were well prepared. Salaried people had been designated to perform the operations vacated by the strike. We didn't have to plan operations around mandatory start times, breaks, and lunch. The flexibility in work schedules allowed productivity to increase, and it increased markedly in some operations.

Dow let it be known the union people weren't missed, and that they might not be needed back. Time ticked by, and the absence of paychecks began to take a toll. The mood on the picket lines darkened a bit more with each passing day.

I was assigned to operate the stainless steel part cleaning line in Building 881. That job didn't require that I dress out for contamination protection. Some desired the "cold" work in 881, but I never felt comfortable working in a building that was several stories deep below ground level. Plant designers decided the building should be built into a hillside, and that would protect it in the event of nuclear attack. I knew a well-placed Russian warhead would have destroyed the building. I never became accustomed to the walk up the steep stairs out of the building at the end of a shift to find there had been snow, or that there was a major wind storm in progress, or that the sun was out and it was the end of a beautiful day. However, the work I was doing was clean and easy. There was no pressure; a few hours of actual work was all that was needed to clean many more parts than required by the schedule. My paychecks kept coming. This was when our daughter was born, and I have plenty of great family memories from this time. It was a much different story for the union members who were on strike. Dow increased the pressure on them by announcing an official decision had been made that only a very few union jobs would be needed to continue plant operations, and anyone who crossed the picket lines to apply for one of those jobs would be given seniority. The strike began to break when some union members began crossing the picket lines.

Word appeared in the news that union leaders had gone to Washington, D.C. to meet with senior AEC officials. They presented and explained what they wanted, and the story I heard was that the AEC directed Dow to agree to what was being asked by the union. I recall that everyone thought that would be the end of the strike, and the union officials were undoubtedly ready to celebrate. The money to pay for higher wages and better benefits would be provided by AEC, and there was no reason for Dow not to agree. But Dow said no. They were said to have told the AEC that salary surveys of the Denver area proved the requested wages and benefits were out of line. AEC told Dow they didn't buy that explanation, and once again directed Dow to agree to the union's demands. Dow responded that they had been contracted by AEC to manage the plant, and negotiating a labor agreement consistent with local labor conditions was part of that management responsibility. AEC could criticize their management decisions and use that criticism in future contract negotiations with Dow, but they couldn't tell Dow how to manage operations.

The union and AEC were undoubtedly astonished at this development. The company plans to only hire back a few union workers progressed. The company position was that a new contract had been offered and refused, and since there was no contract, the company could hire anyone they wanted. Previous rules about work assignments based on the seniority system also were no longer in force. Word spread that even the AEC couldn't force Dow to change their minds, and the number of people crossing the lines began to increase. One worker returned to the area where I was working. I could tell the worker was not happy. It was eventually shared with me that unpaid bills required the return. The mood on the picket lines became black. There were even a few ugly incidents when salaried people stopped in local bars on the way home in the evenings and encountered people who were on strike.

Union officials were apparently becoming desperate, and took desperate action. They went to the media and warned that Rocky Flats was not a safe place without their members working there. Newspapers had front-page stories about how conditions at Rocky Flats were endangering everyone there and the people in the local communities. There were also news reports involving interviews of union officials. In one, the reporter began by saying, "Charges of radioactive pollution against Dow Chemical Company are in the news this afternoon. Striking workers at Dow say the company is letting radioactive pollution into our state." (Transcript of report on KBTR radio, July17, 1970)

These reports astonished me. My first thoughts were that I had great respect for the union people I had worked with, and that I couldn't believe they would condone the tactic of saying anyone who worked there would be willing to work unsafely or allow radioactive pollution to be released into the environment where we lived with our families. I then wondered why anyone who wanted a job at Rocky Flats would want to make people afraid of the place. I don't know that I understood that strikes are always ugly, and that the senior people on both sides will do whatever it takes to win an advantage. Senior officials of the union were only doing what they believed they needed to do. The people I worked with and I weren't worried. We believed people reading the newspapers and seeing television reports or hearing radio interviews would understand that we weren't going to put our families or ourselves at risk. We were wrong. The stories were accepted by at least some, or perhaps many, of the general public as fact.

I don't know whether the reports given to the media about dangers at the site contributed to the eventual settlement of the strike, but a new contract was signed. The perception was that the company won. We heard there was frustration within the AEC toward Dow. Dow was confronted more frequently by the AEC, which wanted more say in management decisions. Dow continued to resist. Workers came back, but things weren't the same. There was anger toward the people who crossed the picket lines and the people such as myself who had done the work while the strike was on. We were all considered "scabs." Another lasting impact of the strike was fallout from using announcements about safety concerns to get what was wanted. Critics protesting Rocky Flats had previously focused on what they believed to be the immorality of building parts for nuclear weapons. The critics learned that talking about the danger created by Rocky Flats was a much more effective tactic. People who weren't impressed with arguments that bombs shouldn't be built did listen to stories of how even the workers were afraid of what was done there, and had said the place was full of people who didn't care about safety. The "safety card" would be played to gain advantage in coming years, but it would be the site owner, the government bureaucracy, that played it to gain more government employees and larger budgets.

I do not criticize those who believed our mission was wrong and protested against what we were doing. I know they were passionate in their beliefs. I also know they disagreed with my willingness to do the work I was doing, and that was and is their right. I didn't appreciate it when they accused those of us who worked at Rocky Flats as caring nothing about safety. That was not true. It was even more difficult to take in the later days when the people who owned the site that we worked for were the ones who made the accusations.

Chapter 7

Transfer to Environmental
or
Changing from Classified to Unclassified Work

The increasing scrutiny from the news media about Rocky Flats resulted in predominantly negative stories. The consistent theme was about the plant's "cloak of secrecy," dangers of what was done there, and inferences and direct allegations about the inadequacy of protection for the people in the area. Information about how to make parts for nuclear weapons was and is carefully guarded as secret. However, the results from environmental monitoring of air, water, and soil on and near the site were never hidden behind a "cloak of secrecy." The results of the extensive monitoring program were widely distributed in public meetings and in unclassified reports.

I was uninformed about environmental programs at Rocky Flats when I worked in the production areas, which illustrates the separation of the many activities performed at the site. The plant was similar to a small city, with the individual buildings representing neighborhoods. The only time I had previously visited the environmental organizations and laboratories in Building 123 was to pick up my radiation dosimeter. Many people worked an entire career in one building. People who worked in 881 seldom had a reason to visit 771, 776, or 991. Part of that was encouraged by the security process for the production areas, because access to those areas was based on "need to know." Just because you had a Q clearance to work in 776 didn't mean you needed to know production secrets about what was being manufactured in other buildings.

My new bosses approached me with a plan to transfer me to the environmental organization. They didn't care that I didn't have any environmental experience. They were under increasing pressure to add emphasis to environmental monitoring and control and to publish more reports about the results. The bosses seemed to think my ability to write (maybe some reading this will question their judgment) qualified me to be one of the new people joining the environmental organization. They made it clear any resistance to a transfer was not going to stop it from happening. The site hired me because of my experience with the nuclear arsenal, and I preferred to stay where the weapons parts were being built instead of moving to the "more honorable" task of monitoring the environment. However, I moved to the Building 123 laboratory within days of being told I was going to transfer.

I quickly learned I had been forced into a wonderful job. There was no change of clothes required to enter contaminated areas, no safes for classified information, and no alarms for alerting that radioactivity had been released. My new coworkers were professional, ethical, and dedicated to accurate and complete monitoring and reporting. The difference between what was being reported by the press and what I saw happening in the new organization was quite remarkable.

The specifics of what I had to learn in my new job were numerous, detailed, and complex. I had moved from a classified world to a technical job requiring collecting and analyzing samples and reporting the results. The previous work was more intriguing, but this new job was challenging and interesting.

The best thing about my new job was that no one seemed to really know what my specific assignment might be. It's the only time in my professional career no one seemed to be telling me what to do, so I looked for activities that seemed interesting and did a little bit of everything. There wasn't a problem finding people to teach me. It was obvious most of the people were happy to show off their knowledge of what they were doing. It seemed they found it as refreshing to have someone wanting to know about their work as it was for me to learn about it. The technicians taught me the techniques and procedures for collecting samples and the chemists taught me the analytical technology. I didn't learn enough to do the work, but I certainly learned enough to appreciate that those people were dedicated and skilled.

One of my favorite tasks was helping sample the ponds downstream of the site, and I frequently volunteered to help with that sampling. My help usually consisted of walking around the ponds looking for fish, frogs, or whatever other critters might be around. I often thought of helping my Grandfathers catch bullheads out of their farm ponds. The first of the ponds had been built on the Rocky Flats site in the early 1950s shortly after production operations began. Additional ponds were added over the years. Those ponds and well-defined waste handling procedures were later judged to have played an important role in reducing plutonium in off-site discharges.

The results of the sampling and analyses were reported monthly, quarterly, and annually to AEC officials, Dow management, representatives from the local cities, the State of Colorado, the U.S. Environmental Protection Agency (EPA), and interested citizens who had asked to be put on the distribution lists. I found reference to sampling of "air, vegetation, water, snow, soil, mud, algae, and wildlife" to establish "normal background" for Rocky Flats and the environment by an organization called "Site Survey" in 1952 before production operations began. (Edward A. Putzier, Preface)

Monthly meetings were held to discuss the environmental monitoring results and independent results from the cities, State, and EPA. There had been an agreement signed between the Energy Research and Development Administration (ERDA) the governmental agency that replaced the AEC, EPA, and the State that funded the cities to establish monitoring programs with EPA assistance and oversight. I was interested in water sampling results from the City of Broomfield on samples from both Great Western Reservoir and their treated drinking water, which was the water used by my family. The chemists from Broomfield invariably reported that the water met all drinking water standards, which confirmed the results reported by the site.

Both Great Western Reservoir and Standley Lake had been used for irrigation until several years after Rocky Flats began operations. Low-level concentrations of radioactive materials had been measured and reported in the sediments of both lakes when Great Western was converted to drinking water supply by Broomfield in 1962 and Standley Lake was converted to provide drinking water for Westminster, Thornton, and Northglenn in 1966. (ChemRisk, August 1992, pages 181 and 184) The good news is that plutonium is extremely insoluble, so virtually none of what was in the sediment made it into the drinking water. The drinking water provided by the two lakes as measured by the various independent agencies did not exceed standards for radioactive materials.

There were seldom if ever discrepancies in the comparison of analytical results by Rocky Flats, the cities, and the regulators. Critical members of the public who chose to attend the open meetings often expressed concerns, and those would be answered freely and without restriction. Sampling efforts were continually reviewed and expanded over the years. The only constant was the contention by critics that not enough was being done. Those comments weren't ignored, and the environmental monitoring programs were frequently expanded as a result.

There were occasional allegations or inferences that monitoring results that would be embarrassing to the site were kept secret. One of my assignments was helping assemble the data and calculate the final results into tables for inclusion in the routine reports. The analytical results came straight to me after validation by the quality control people. No one ever asked, suggested, or directed that any of the validated data be excluded, ignored, or hidden. I would have been astonished if that had ever happened. The people in the laboratory were simply too honest and dedicated to the work to even contemplate such actions. We told

22

management if we found anything out of the ordinary, and I never heard a manager suggest or direct that validated data should be excluded from reporting. I often would investigate why we had a result that was elevated above what was normally found. I would write reports about the investigation and results. I understand the files from Rocky Flats include many, maybe even dozens, of such reports that were written because I had some curiosity about some aspect of the monitoring. Any and all results that prompted these internal investigations were included in the routine reports that were distributed to anyone interested and discussed at the monthly meetings, called the "State Exchange Meeting." No one ever told me to stop researching and reporting.

I'm proud of my association with the environmental work done by the people at Rocky Flats, and will always appreciate that time in my working life. I also feel a fond connection with the magnificent high mountain prairie that surrounded the site. There was a beautiful valley north of the industrial area where there was a deserted house and barn called the Lindsey Ranch. I often found reason to visit the pond near the house on the excuse we needed some background water samples. I visited this peaceful place many times, but never entered any of the buildings. I felt that would be an unacceptable intrusion on the privacy of the people who had lived there and had been evicted when the decision was made to build the Rocky Flats Plant. I often stopped at the edge of the plateau above the ranch to enjoy the view. One day I saw a lone coyote staring back at me from near the pond. I remembered stories of how Native Americans believed some places are sacred. I felt as if I were an interloper, and left the coyote to keep the watch. I hope the bicycle and hiking trails that are planned now that Rocky Flats is a wildlife refuge don't go down into the valley, but I also hope I can go back to the edge of that plateau after the wildlife refuge is opened.

Chapter 8

Public Relations Projects

or

Hopeless Attempts to Create Positive News Reports

The people I met while working to build parts for nuclear weapons didn't spend much time worrying that some in society were critical of their occupations. I continued to have contact with people working the production lines after my transfer to the environmental group. I also had contact with a few engineers from the places where the weapons were designed. There also were occasional visits from military people who were the caretakers of the nuclear arsenal. I recall few, if any, of these people believed there was anything wrong with building and stockpiling weapons with the funds provided by each successive Congress. I think I could say the Rocky Flats employees, at the usual risk of generalizing, believed they were loyal citizens doing important work. However, there was a growing sense of discomfort by the early 1970s. The negative publicity following the 1969 fire combined with reports that people working at the site had no interest in safety resulted in an increasing number of unfavorable stories on television and in newspapers.

The unfavorable impression wasn't just at Rocky Flats; there was growing sentiment around the country questioning the need for nuclear weapons, or at least the need for more of them. Even the name of the Atomic Energy Commission (AEC) made people uncomfortable. The name was changed from AEC to Energy Research and Development Agency (ERDA), which eliminated the negative word "Atomic." The agency name was later changed to Department of Energy (DOE), which of course is a more favorable sounding acronym. But simply changing names wasn't enough. There were attempts within the AEC to find peacetime uses for nuclear weapons. Operation Plowshare was born "…to find practical industrial and scientific uses for nuclear explosives." There really were numerous "excavation" projects considered, including making a new canal across the Isthmus of Panama and a new harbor at Cape Thompson, Alaska. (Sandia National Laboratories, April 2001) The underground explosions designed to improve natural gas extraction was the selected use, but approval was held up until the Soviets resumed nuclear weapon testing in the summer of 1964, breaking a test-ban treaty, and plans for Plowshare moved forward. (DOE, 1996)

My favorite trivia question about Rocky Flats goes something like this, "How many nuclear devices that had plutonium parts built at Rocky Flats have been detonated in Colorado?"

Most people scoff and say something such as, "That's stupid! There haven't been any!"

There were four. One was a single device detonated underground under the name of Project Rulison. There were three detonated within microseconds of each other for Project Rio Blanco. I believe parts for both projects came from Rocky Flats (and I may even have had some involvement with the parts for Rio Blanco). The blasts were intended to fracture "tight geologic formations" that were rich in natural gas.

Those blasts in Colorado weren't the first Plowshare detonations. (Note that the information to follow was gathered mostly from the National Technical Information Service (NTIS) web site.) The first "shot" was a 3-kiloton nuclear device detonated December 10, 1961 at a depth of 1,184 feet east of Carlsbad in New Mexico This test was cleverly called Gnome, because the yield was small compared to future planned tests. The second phase of the project, which was to be called Coach, was never performed. The part of the project named Coach apparently was intended to prove the blast hadn't vented, but the blast did vent with contamination being released (NTIS, January, 2002).

There was another experiment named Gasbuggy that took place in New Mexico, about 55 miles east of Farmington and about 600 feet deep. It was a 29-kiloton device detonated on the sixth anniversary of Gnome. Evidently there was no evidence of venting from Gasbuggy (NTIS, January 1995, September 1996, and December 2000).

The next two projects are the origin of my trivia question about nuclear device detonations in Colorado (note that they weren't called atomic bombs, because that they weren't considered weapons). A 43-kiloton device was detonated about 8,426 feet deep for Project Rulison (NTIS August 1996 and Denver Post, January 29, 2006 and February 12, 2007). The next project, called Rio Blanco, used three 30-kiloton devices placed at about 5,900, 6,300, and 6,900 feet underground in an area north of Rulison (NTIS, December 2001).

The Rulison detonation worked as planned. The blast occurred, and there was a nice, big hole underground with no releases to the atmosphere. However, Rio Blanco wasn't a total success. There were questions raised before the tests as to whether the three blasts would generate earthquakes or vent radioactive gases. The project people assured everyone they had studied the geology of the area thoroughly and nothing could possibly go wrong. The first blast would be the deepest device, and the hole and cracking would form a chimney with the two holes on top after the shallower blasts occurred in sequence. The blasts occurred as planned, no gases were vented, but the chimney didn't form. There were separate holes in the rock. Samples were collected of the gases in the underground holes at all the projects, and the results brought unwelcome news. The gas was too radioactive to be used (NTIS, December 2001). It would take a very long time for the radioactive decay to be sufficient for the gas to be usable. The Colorado legislature then outlawed future nuclear detonations in the state.

The recent interest in energy created by price spikes has led a Texas company to apply for permits to drill natural gas wells as close as 900 feet to where the Rulison shot was detonated. The Department of Energy is considering the project, speculating that the radioactive materials from the detonation will be trapped by the rock that was melted into glass from the intense heat (Denver Post, January 20, 2005, page 4A).

High-level AEC officials weren't the only people who noticed that Rocky Flats and other nuclear weapon component manufacturing sites were developing bad reputations. There were at least a few, perhaps many, Rocky Flats workers who were worried about the news reports and the questions from their family and neighbors. They knew they and their coworkers weren't behaving irresponsibly, but perhaps believed the negative stories were about people in buildings they had never visited.

The methodology for writing a press report about Rocky Flats began to be well developed in the early 1970s. Headlines for the articles contained words such as "secret" and "dangerous". Those words would be supplanted or supplemented with words such as "spewing" or "radiotoxic," and the standard recipe for reports about Rocky Flats became established. I don't remember the word "laced" being used very often in stories about Rocky Flats, although it is a popular word used in writing environmental stories designed to elicit negative reactions.

The downward slope of Rocky Flats' reputation became increasingly frustrating for the people in the environmental group. Discussions around the coffee pot more frequently focused on the negative press, although the Broncos never fell out of being the number one subject during football season. The discussions naturally had many people thinking how we could improve our reputation. I shared an office with one of those people, and one day there was an excited announcement. He advocated that we could create a positive press story if we rescued prairie dogs being threatened by development and transplant them to establish a colony in the Rocky Flats buffer zone. Management loved the idea. Arrangements were made with a local fire department to flush the prairie dogs out of their holes. Cardboard boxes of wet prairie dogs began to arrive in our office in the evening and were put near the heater. The rodents that survived the night were in for an interesting day. My office partner and one of the laboratory technicians loaded them in the back of a pickup and drove them to the high mountain prairie south of the Rocky Flats industrial area. Each living prairie dog was placed in a hole dug manually by the laboratory technician with a posthole digger.

A mystery developed. Several batches of the animals had been planted over several days, but the prairie dog-planting team wouldn't find any prairie dogs the next morning. They drove around searching for signs of the critters, thinking the animals didn't trust their new holes and had moved during the night. Nothing was found. Eventually it was noticed there were two coyotes closely watching the transplant area, and a tall snow fence successfully protected the prairie dogs. The press was called, photographs were taken, and everyone with the exception of a neighboring rancher was happy. The rancher threatened a lawsuit if the rodents moved onto his property. The prairie dog experiment quietly came to an end. The snow fence around the new colony was removed, and the prairie dogs disappeared.

Another project intended to be used for public relations was acquisition of a mobile air monitoring van. The intent was to equip the van with instrumentation that would sample and analyze air for pollutants included in the Clean Air Act. Those pollutants had little to do with Rocky Flats, except for emissions from all the cars entering and leaving the place, but the idea was that school kids would love to see how the monitoring was performed. The public debut of the van was in the parking lot of a shopping mall in Boulder, Colorado. I heard the few people who came near the van would typically eye the big "Rocky Flats Mobile Air Monitoring Van" sign on the side. Those that stayed would ask suspicious questions about what had been released from the site. I also heard that people usually hurriedly hustled away with their children before a full explanation could be given that the van wasn't there as part of some emergency response.

Chapter 9

The Tritium Release

or

An Unwise Approach to Improving Public Image

One of the locations where water was collected by the State of Colorado independent of Rocky Flats was at the culvert where Walnut Creek flowed under Indiana Street on its way to Great Western Reservoir. The CDH laboratory analyzed the water for the logical contaminants, such as plutonium, uranium, and americium. They also analyzed for tritium. Rocky Flats didn't sample and analyze for tritium, and didn't even have the instrumentation to do that analysis, because processing that radioactive isotope of hydrogen wasn't part of the site's mission.

One day a call came from CDH reporting their laboratory had a high tritium result in a sample from the Walnut Creek sampling location. This report created confusion and concern in the environmental monitoring organization. A Rocky Flats manager called CDH and told them they should check their results. It was suggested they must have allowed their sample to be contaminated with something that had given a false positive for tritium, since Rocky Flats didn't process tritium. CDH collected more samples, and the results were high again.

Concern began to increase. It was learned that Colorado State University, the college that performed many environmental studies of the Rocky Flats ecology, had the instrumentation required to perform tritium analysis. Samples were collected, driven to Fort Collins, and analyzed. The results confirmed high levels of tritium. Rocky Flats stopped adamantly insisting there wasn't any tritium, bought the equipment needed to perform tritium analyses, and began looking for the source of the radioactive hydrogen. There was even talk of whether someone could have "spiked" the water at Walnut Creek with tritium to make us look bad. That didn't seem to be very likely, since tritium isn't all that readily available.

The local media reported news of finding tritium in water leaving Rocky Flats. I heard one television reporter begin a story with an announcement "Tritanium has been detected in water samples from Rocky Flats." One unfortunate aspect of this incident was that tritium results were reported using picocuries as the unit of measure. Pico means one trillionth, and was routinely used in reporting the very tiny amounts of plutonium, uranium, and americium found in environmental samples. Tritium is more typically reported in microcuries, and that unit is a millionth of a curie. The public probably would not have been as concerned if they had heard there was one microcurie of tritium per liter of water found. They were concerned that a million picocuries were found. The two numbers represent an identical amount, just different units of measure. Sort of like someone saying the recipe required a million grains of sugar instead of listing a cup of sugar. (And no, I'm not trying to pass off radioactive hydrogen as being anything like sugar.)

Health department officials were trying to reassure the public the levels of tritium found weren't a health risk; drinking water standards had not been exceeded. I recall a television reporter interviewing a Broomfield citizen.

"Officials say there isn't any risk to drinking the water. How do you feel about that?"

"Well, they say there are millions of picocuries of the stuff in every liter. If a million of anything fell on you, it would be bound to hurt."

There was significant concern about the source of the tritium contamination. Why had there been that much tritium at Rocky Flats, which didn't have the facilities to handle that material? The environmental organization worked overtime collecting and analyzing samples with the newly acquired equipment. Virtually all the water samples from around the site had high tritium results, and that wasn't useful in tracking down the source. A call came from the manager that had hired me to work at Rocky Flats to suggest we should sample a glove box line where some material shipped from an ERDA laboratory in California had been processed. I went to the building, collected samples from a water trap on the line, and the very high results confirmed the suspicion. This is where the tritium originated. The material from California had contained tritium, and when the material was processed, the gaseous tritium went up the stack. The Final Environmental Impact Statement (EIS) for Rocky Flats says, "…the processing of metal scrap contaminated with tritium in 1973 led to the release of several hundred curies of tritium to the air and Plant waste streams." The total release was estimated to range from 100 to 500 curies. There was rain about the same time, the tritium gas exchanged with the regular hydrogen in the rain, and the tritiated water with those millions of picocuries fell all over the Rocky Flats area. The result was that Great Western Reservoir had about 12,000 picocuries per liter of tritium (ERDA EIS, April 1980, pages 2-92 and 3-50). The EPA drinking water standard of 20,000 picocuries per liter for beta emitters such as tritium was passed in 1976, or about three years after the tritium release.

The site ERDA manager gathered everyone who had participated in the search for the tritium source in the Building 111 conference room for a briefing. The official talked about results of the completed tritium release investigation.

"What we found was that ERDA lost control of material. That material should never have been sent here. This incident resulted from a breakdown in ERDA, and Dow was found to be blameless in this matter. Now, we're going to call the press in and brief them. You may stay and listen, but you will not participate."

There were about a dozen reporters in attendance at the briefing that followed. There was nothing mentioned about a breakdown in ERDA being the cause of the incident. The first question following the briefing was, "Is this tritium release the reason Dow's contract to manage Rocky Flats isn't being renewed?"

The official replied, "I don't see any profit to discussing the blame for this."

I was stunned. Every reporter in the room received the clear message that Dow was leaving Rocky Flats because of the tritium release, despite ERDA officials telling Dow employees the company was found blameless by the investigation. I had been in meetings days previously where it was explained why Dow managers had decided not to re-bid the contract. ERDA wanted a company that would operate the plant based on its decisions and a company that would have better relations with the union. Dow wasn't interested in being the contractor with ERDA making the decisions, and that proved to be very wise.

The tritium incident had nothing to do with Dow leaving Rocky Flats, but ERDA intentionally allowed the press, and therefore the people who read or heard reports from those members of the press, to believe that was the reason. Evidently some bureaucrats aren't governed by standards for truthful behavior.

In retrospect, Dow managers made a brilliant decision to not bid on a contract extension. There is no doubt Rockwell executives who managed Rocky Flats according to direction from ERDA (and later DOE) wish they had told ERDA officials they also weren't interested in being the contactor under the conditions demanded by ERDA. Unfortunately for Rockwell, they put together a bid package that promised they would let ERDA make the management decisions with Rockwell carrying out the actions required to implement the decisions. Perhaps the Rockwell executives really didn't understand that ERDA would make the decisions, take credit when things went well, and blame Rockwell when things went poorly. I'm confident Rockwell initially considered they had "won" the contract. I'm guessing Rockwell eventually considered the award to be one of the worst things, maybe the worst thing, that ever happened to the company.

My employment as a Dow Rocky Flats employee ended at this time, and I was pleased to be leaving. I had lost respect for ERDA, and was pleased to be separating from them. Dow Chemical had offered me an environmental consulting job with a new venture in Knoxville, Tennessee. They moved my family and me to Knoxville, where we enjoyed living for the next seven years. I mostly forgot about what was going on at Rocky Flats.

Chapter 10

Returning to Rocky Flats

or

"You Can Check Out Any Time You Like, But You Can Never Leave"

Rockwell Rocky Flats began a hiring frenzy in the early 1980s at the direction of DOE. A call came to me in Tennessee inquiring whether I would be interested in returning to Colorado to a production support job at the Flats. The salary and benefits sounded right, so a combination interview/house hunting trip was arranged. One under-appreciated benefit of living in Colorado was obvious as we were walking down the steps that summer day from the plane onto the tarmac at Stapleton International Airport. It was late evening, just after sundown, and the evening cooling of the low humidity air had already kicked in. Tennessee is a beautiful state, but you don't feel cool, low humidity air there very often if ever. I think we knew during the walk down the steps we were returning to Colorado, and I was returning to Rocky Flats.

Moving a family is never easy, and our departure from Tennessee and return to Colorado had the usual issues. The World Fair had just ended in Knoxville, and a series of unfortunate economic events resulted in a local depression. We couldn't sell our home. Our son was thrilled to be returning to Colorado, but our daughter was unhappy about leaving her friends. We took a long time to select our new permanent home. We hadn't decided on where we wanted to live by the time we moved, so we rented a home while we continued to search. This is a pertinent part of my story, because the only considerations in our search for a home were neighborhood, price, and style. We eventually bought a home (where I am sitting as I type this) in Westminster, CO that is directly in the path of the dominant wind direction from where Rocky Flats was. It never occurred to me that my family would be at any risk at this location. Remember this is coming from the person who had previously assembled all the data from emissions and environmental monitoring programs and prepared and issued the routine reports that included the results.

I wonder whether any skeptics will give any credibility to what I just wrote. Will they continue to believe there was "disposal of excess plutonium from secret vents at Rocky Flats?" Will they believe a person who would have been quite likely to know the truth because of broad experience in both environmental monitoring and production would put his family at risk by moving them into a home in the direction that "excess plutonium" would be carried during high winds? For that matter, would they think I would even be willing to move my family from a good life in

Tennessee to work in the despicable situation they imagined? I can assure you I would never have considered returning with my family if I had any suspicion Rocky Flats was engaged in the activities believed by some.

It is certain the return to the Flats was eerie. I parked in the Building 111 lot and walked toward the east doors. The feeling of déjà vu was overwhelming. It was as if part of my soul had been left behind and had re-entered me. That was the first time I thought of the line from the song, "Hotel California." "You can check out any time you like, but you can never leave."

As an aside, this is as good a place as any to begin to refer to buildings at the Flats the way long-time workers talked. They never said, "Building 111". They said "Eleven Building." Buildings 771, 881, and 991 were "71, 81, and 91." The only change was when the new 371/374 and 460 buildings were constructed. They were referenced in conversation by the full numbers.

Parking and walking into 11 weren't the only two experiences recreated. I was once again logged in as an uncleared worker. I inquired how long a wait I might expect to get my clearance renewed, and was told I had been gone long enough (more than five years) that a new investigation, including background check, would be required. I believe my comment, "You'll probably find my childhood hasn't changed," is the reason the second clearance process took longer than the first.

One difference from my first wait for a clearance was that this time I was being housed in a trailer full of uncleared people. The other people were recent college graduates. I wasn't given anything to do, except for some encouragement to "brush up on technical things." Brushing up on technical things couldn't include any classified documents, since I didn't have a clearance.

The next three months seemed to be endless. I read all manner of journals, and some were actually about chemistry, physics, or other sciences. I kept those handy to put over National Geographic, Newsweek, and the Wall Street Journal when the "scout" gave a warning. The scout was the person assigned to watch out the window and warn us to look busy when "the spy from Personnel" came to check and verify we were "being productive." The "scout" assignment was pretty boring, so we all took our turn. This didn't seem to be a great environment to break in a group consisting mostly of new college graduates beginning their first professional employment.

Another negative for people new to Rocky Flats was the number and frequency of protests and routine nature of derogatory news reports. The focus of both protests and many news reports was on risks from the place instead of the morality of what was being made.

Reading journals of any kind several hours a day could not fill up a workday. I decided walking around unclassified areas of the site and talking to the several people I had worked with previously could also be considered "productive." Something was needed to fill in the day as I waited for my clearance to be re-approved. I happened across one of my previous coworkers from the environmental group. We exchanged pleasantries, and I ventured, "I'm still waiting to get my clearance back, but can you tell me why there are so many new people being hired?"

"Yeah, they're getting ready for the big layoff."

As things turned out, the prediction was correct, but was made about twenty years early.

My security clearance finally was renewed, and I made my way back to 79, the same building where I had worked after receiving my clearance the first time. This time I didn't need an escort. I enjoyed getting reacquainted with people in the research and development staff, and there hadn't been that much change in personnel considering I had been gone several years. One of my first stops was in the office of the plutonium production manager, another person I had worked with previously. "Things have changed since you left. We hire a person to do some work and DOE hires ten people to try to stop it. The other day we had the Fire Department down to try and re-start an area they had shut down. We kept suggesting things we could do to meet their requirements. One of them accused us of 'just looking for ways to re-start the operation.' Funny thing, they accused me, the person responsible for plutonium production, of looking for ways to meet their requirements and operate an area needed to complete production schedules."

My assignment to supporting plutonium production was a dream job. There was complete freedom to walk the production areas and talk to people about problems they might be having. My primary assignment was to identify what the research organization could do to help if there were problems. It was quickly apparent anyone who acted as if they were willing to help was treated well after trust was gained that I wasn't some sort of "undercover auditor."

I received a call from a young engineer who explained he had been assigned to have a new piece of machinery installed in a glove box to replace an out-of-date machine. The engineer had heard I helped someone get something done, and was desperate to find help. "My boss says he's going to fire me if I don't get this installed, and everyone just keeps giving me reasons why it can't be done."

"What stops it from being installed?"

"The base was cast in a honeycomb to reduce weight, and the criticality engineers say it can't be bolted on the floor of the glove box until the empty spaces are filled with something."

"Why would that matter?"

"They say some liquid might wick up into the holes and change the criticality configuration."

"O.K. Why don't you fill the holes with something?"

"No one will approve anything we suggest. Everything is rejected by the people who have to approve things put into the lines."

I promised I'd try to help, and began making the rounds of places where I had previously found people who had both the experience and willingness to solve problems. One stop was in the 78-maintenance area, and I found one of the helpful people. I had learned previously that a trickle of tobacco juice on a person's chin doesn't diminish, and might even improve, the ability to solve problems such as this one. The worker was well aware of the problem.

"Yeah, we've been trying to get that thing put in the line for months. Funny thing is, we've done stuff like this several times before."

"What's different this time?"

"Nobody seems to know. Every time someone makes a suggestion there are several people who won't approve it."

"How did you handle it those earlier times?"

"We filled the holes with this stuff," pointing at a 55-gallon drum. The label and instructions claimed the epoxy hardened quickly to be as strong as steel.

I said something like, "I wonder why they don't just use that again?"

My intentions were honorable. I left a message for the young engineer that I intended to find how to get the "liquid steel" approved to seal the holes in his piece of equipment. I began making calls to people who approved materials for the lines. The material would react and harden before the equipment would be put into the lines. Certainly, I reasoned, that couldn't cause any unwanted chemical vapors to get into the lines. I answered the phone a couple of days into this search for information, and was peppered with several accusations posed in the form of questions. It seems the maintenance people had filled the holes in the base of the piece of equipment with the "liquid steel" and installed the equipment in the glove box after the epoxy hardened.

"We're trying to find out who authorized this."

"Authorized what?"

"Using the epoxy."

"What was supposed to happen?"

We had a committee of ten people who were supposed to sign off on whatever was done."

"Hmmm."

"Now what are we supposed to do? We can't take it out, because it's installed and contaminated."

"Hmmm."

"When we asked the crew who authorized this, they say they don't know the name, but it was 'some big guy'."

"Hmmm."

Gaining a reputation for being a problem-solver had a down side. I was forced to take a management position. I didn't cave in easily. I laughed at them when they told me about the "power and prestige" of management. They attempted to counter my laughter by reminding me the organization I would manage would have the world's third largest stockpile of the plutonium pits (behind the United States and Russia), not to mention one of the largest collections of classified reports. My response was to laugh at them again, and ask what power and prestige can be gained from something that can't be discussed. The next approach was for them to claim that I would be more challenged or I would be able to learn more. I rejected that approach also, although I would later learn they hadn't been exaggerating; there would be frequent contact with the people and agencies where weapons were designed.

The quest to promote me continued; I recall rejecting the offer eight or nine times before I was told it was my duty and responsibility to the take the job. "We don't want to have to give the job to an outsider, and you're the only person in the group that doesn't have a long history of rejecting management positions." The honesty was too much for me to resist, and I accepted. I admit it didn't occur to me at the time that I now, by becoming a manager, had become even less trustworthy to the outside world.

Chapter 11

The New Rocky Flats

or

Individual Expertise Is Replaced By Bureaucracy

The approach of the end of the Cold War changed things at Rocky Flats. There were fewer plutonium pits being produced by many more people. The plutonium production manager hadn't exaggerated the numbers of people assigned to "audit", "evaluate", or perhaps to be more honest, to criticize. A good day for the internal critics was a day they could document something that needed improvement. This would be an excellent approach for a normal business; everyone should want to find methods to make things safer and more efficient.

Unfortunately, parts of the equation that would have existed in a commercial business were missing at Rocky Flats. Processes were rigorously controlled, and there was no incentive to gain improvements in productivity and efficiency. The budget was available to fund all the paychecks and infrastructure. Once production was no longer the guiding purpose of the plant, people began seeking promotions or building fiefdoms through other means. The favorite means was analyzing activities and processes and criticizing the adequacy of safety of the operations and/or written procedures. Operations had to be changed and new procedures had to be written. The critics could then analyze, criticize, and require a new set of changes. Detailed training was required with each change.

Operations with flawless safety records weren't immune. Auditors were continually finding things "that might go wrong," and requiring other people to respond and find a solution. I offered a simplistic idea for responding when an expert in some safety specialty found that an operation needed improvement. I suggested the expert finding the problem be assigned the task of identifying solutions to the problem. Not a chance. The experts had to be free from problem solving to allow more time to identify additional problems. Holding "problem finders" separate from becoming part of the solution was judged to improve their independence.

Improving safety became an ever-expanding industry at Rocky Flats. It also became apparent that self-criticism resulted in larger project budgets. Unfortunately, someone should have established limits on this elegant approach to getting budget requests approved. The flood of self-critical reports was attracting the attention of the Justice Department and resulted in journalists voting Rocky Flats being "...besieged by problems" as the top news story for Colorado for the year 1988. (Sunday Camera, January 1, 1989)

The emphasis on self-criticism brought in more money to budgets, but it also caused significant changes in the work areas. Operations that had been successfully completed by skilled individuals were changed to rely on increasingly complex procedures and validation processes. Individual expertise is difficult to quantify, and a critic could easily find fault. I will use the example of the "backyard mechanic" fitting a precision-machined screw fitting into a tapped recess with equally tight tolerances. The experienced person gently inserts the screw into the recess, and slowly rotates it back and forth until the sense of feel in concert with the best of all computers, the human mind, signals everything is aligned. The screw can then be tightened into the recess without risk of stripping the threads. This backyard mechanic approach was an aberration in a culture where there is no value given to skill and experience. There would be a massive effort to either think of ways to document the process in procedures, and when that failed there would be an effort to use machines to reproduce the process. Regardless of the approach, there would be little if any chance the new procedures or automation would be as successful as when that skilled backyard mechanic was doing the work.

Expertise that had worked for decades was replaced by detailed procedures. There were large increases in staffing as more and more people were watching the operators and filling out forms. Not a bad approach if you really don't need to produce anything and there is an unlimited amount of taxpayer money to pay the salaries regardless of how the time is used.

Of course morale declined as appreciation for individual skills was replaced by bureaucracy. I was working with one of the hourly people in a production area, and was surprised by the level of anger being expressed. I finally said something such as, "You sound as if this place makes you miserable. Have you thought of looking for a different job?" The worker looked at me incredulously, and then said something I will interpret to be, "Are you crazy? How could someone at my age and salary ever replace this job?" The questions were heavily interspersed with expletives.

One of my favorite series of news reports during this time came from a local television station. The series had a title including the description "Investigative Reports," and the name "Rocky Flats". Every night for a week a new story began with "Our investigation revealed…"

I believe the reports were being taken from the impact statement about the site that had been issued by DOE in 1980. The three-volume document contains a complete description of everything unclassified that would be of interest about the first three decades of Rocky Flats operations, including details about accidents. (DOE, April 1980, Section 3.2) Of course the source of the information didn't make reports about accidents involving fires and spills of radioactive materials any less sensational.

There was a person in the research organization that was approaching retirement during this time. I pulled the personnel files and began to consider what could be said at the farewell dinner planned to honor his career. I was astonished to find this person had been massively contaminated in the 1950s by a pipe leaking plutonium nitrate solution. The soluble, acidified plutonium wouldn't wash off, and this person lived for a week in the medical department wrapped in plastic to "sweat out the contamination." If anyone had the right to be skeptical of safety at Rocky Flats, this had to be that person.

"Don't you resent what happened?"

"No, not at all. I knew there were risks, accepted them, and am happy with the outcome."

"Aren't you worried there might be long-term health implications?"

"Nope. No reason to worry about what I can't control. It happened long ago, and nothing has shown up yet."

"Don't all the stories about how this place puts people into unacceptable risk concern you?"

"Nope. Look, when I came here I was working at an ice cream factory where working conditions were really dangerous. And I tripled my salary when I came here. Now I'm retiring with a generous retirement package and lifetime health insurance. One unfortunate accident that resulted in me being uncomfortable for a week isn't that big a deal in a 30-year plus career of working in a safe, comfortable, lucrative place."

"Why would an ice cream factory be unsafe?"

"Mixers and open vats everywhere. Not uncommon for people to lose fingers or even hands. The nickname "stubby" had to be followed by a last name, or you wouldn't know which of the many was being mentioned."

Not everyone was as willing to understand as this remarkable person. In fact, things took a really interesting turn when DOE decided to capitalize on the effectiveness of self-criticism. The numbers of people in DOE organizations began to increase as reports were frequently issued with words such as "The assessment found..." followed by the recommendation "Oversight needs to be increased."

There was an announcement in the last half of 1987 that DOE intended to bring in a group of experts to perform a radiation safety appraisal of Building 71. The group of people brought an impressive list of titles and credentials. The review of processes, procedures, operations, and records of results was said to have been impressively well organized and detailed. There was trepidation about where this would lead, but the out-briefing was complimentary. There were words such as, "Although some operations are not performed exactly in concert with procedural requirements, the results are encouraging. Incidents of contamination are quite infrequent, detected quickly, and corrected effectively and efficiently."

As far as I know, the evaluation and conclusions were never finalized for publication. People at the site were confident that nothing had changed when the same team of people returned a few short months later and began performing a similar appraisal. That confidence was reinforced when DOE announced they were extending Rockwell's contract with a statement, "Rockwell's overall performance is vastly improved since 1985, said (a) DOE spokesman...." (Boulder Daily Camera, March 5, 1988, page 1A)

The confidence was unwarranted, to understate what happened. There was a scathing report issued discussing how the site's contamination control practices were unacceptable. A news article published 15 days after Rockwell's contract was extended with the compliment that Rockwell's performance had significantly improved said, "Sloppy work habits, faulty equipment, and lax attitudes have created 'significant safety concerns' at Rocky Flats...." (Rocky Mountain News, March 20, 1988, page 6)   Another article elaborated, "....DOE must provide significant improvements in the radiation protection and safety programs to meet current, and future, technical, engineering, and scientific procedures and practices for controlling sources and contamination, performing external and internal dosimetry, and implementing accident response including applicable protective action guides. The culture of safety is not yet well established at Rocky Flats. The philosophy of the Department of Energy and the management of Rocky Flats is not understood, accepted, and believed by the work force." (NTIS, November 1991)

Another document listing events in the history of Rocky Flats made a much simpler statement. It said, "A U.S. DOE safety appraisal of the plant is highly critical of safety procedures and recommends major changes." (Kaiser-Hill/DOE, 2003)

The news media enjoyed a wonderful opportunity for sensational front-page news. Politicians issued statements about sloppy work at Rocky Flats endangering surrounding areas. The normal human tendency is to try to play down problems. The perception was that everything must be on the verge of disaster for such a negative appraisal to be issued by the owner of the site. We at the site were baffled, since there hadn't been a contamination incident between the time of the first audit, the extension of Rockwell's contract, and the second audit.

Much of the criticism in the audit referred to the process followed by workers in checking themselves and their clothing for contamination when exiting the "hot" areas. There were machines called "combos" at each exit where every worker was required to screen booties, hands, face, and coveralls for contamination. The good news is that the machines reacted quickly and obviously to contamination by a series of loud clicks, or a buzz if there were higher levels. Workers had been successfully "frisking" themselves with these machines for decades, and reports of anyone found to have left the area with undetected contamination were very, very scarce. (I did hear one rumor, which I can't confirm, about a worker wearing contaminated clothing home, and it was said his wife wasn't impressed that she had to be decontaminated.) There were strong individual incentives for workers to adequately screen for contamination. No one would want to take contamination home to their family.

Skepticism about the validity of the negative reports became rampant in the work force when word spread that the report said people were not rigorously following procedural instructions. It was learned that much of the criticism was based on failure to follow instructions defining the sequence to be followed in checking the booties and hands with the combos. Monitoring the left hand first when the procedure prescribed monitoring the right hand first had no impact on the success of the "frisking" in finding contamination, but it was judged to be a procedure violation. Some people were also observed monitoring the left bootie first instead of starting with the right bootie as prescribed by the procedure. Also, the monitoring wands were moved too fast to be in compliance with procedure. Workers had learned over decades of experience the detectors reacted quickly if there was contamination. However, moving the wand faster than the procedure prescribed, even though it would still clearly detect and respond to contamination, was judged to be a violation.

Management quickly responded to the growing unrest among the workers over what they judged to be a "DOE witch hunt." DOE took the growing skepticism to be proof, "The culture of safety…is not understood, accepted, and believed by the work force." Senior Rockwell managers spread out to brief workers that resistance to corrective actions would not be accepted. The director of my organization told us, "Procedures are being rewritten, and will be fully implemented immediately."

Others and I protested that the rewriting of the procedures should involve watching how the workers were successfully finding contamination and using those observations to rewrite the procedures. Certainly, we asserted, the objective must be to continue the successes being experienced by the workers in finding and containing contamination. Several of us said it would surprise us if anyone could be found who knew more about contamination control than the Rocky Flats workers.

"DOE has endorsed our approach, and is requiring us to implement it. It won't be changed. Look, we all have to support this. One of the strongest criticisms is that we at the site are resisting required improvements."

I responded by saying, "I can only say that the requirement for improvement is questionable, since I haven't heard of any recent records of failure."

"Look, we will be required to implement the changes. And the policy will be that workers not following the new procedure will be fired and their manager replaced."

"So why will we punish the workers and reward the managers?"

My boss evidently thought enough of my past performance that I wasn't fired. The new procedures were written and put into practice. People grudgingly followed them verbatim. They monitored their hands and feet in the required sequence. They moved the monitoring probe over their bodies and clothing at the snail pace specified. The managers (including me) stood at the combos and made checklists documenting procedural compliance by the people monitoring themselves. There was a continuation of the identical lack of contamination incidents that had preceded these changes. However, politicians who had been critical of the site began voting to increase funding to sponsor even more changes. It had been proven once again that self-criticism brought in additional funding and allowed more oversight people to be hired. This series of events and the flow of additional money to the site would be virtually inconsequential in comparison to what would happen in the future.

I have wondered what would have happened if the vote on an amendment that read in part, "Shall the constitution of the State of Colorado be amended in order to bring about the cessation of nuclear weapons component production in Colorado..." had happened in 1988 or later. The amendment was defeated 584,356 to 326,550 in 1982. (Rocky Mountain News, November 4, 1982)

Chapter 12

Return to Environmental
or
In Retrospect, Not My Best Decision

The good news was that the reductions in efficiency didn't make any difference, because the production schedules were constantly dwindling. The economic and technical power displayed by the United States in producing an overwhelmingly well-armed military convinced the Soviet Union they could not win. My opinion is that capitalism prevailed. We could fund the huge costs of the Cold War and still remain a wealthy country. The Soviets couldn't.

That simple explanation about why the Cold War ended is undoubtedly incomplete; there are complex assessments that either free world political policy, flaws in the Soviet system, or a combination of the two caused the dissolution of the Soviet Union. However, it was indisputable that Rocky Flats wasn't going to be needed to produce plutonium pits, or at least not in very large quantities.

The people working at the site certainly didn't realize the production mission was coming to an end as early as the people in Washington did. Perhaps we would have felt better if we had been part of the planning to convert the mission from production to safety. However, the plan, if it was a conscious plan, hadn't been officially announced. The days began to be filled with mindless, verbatim compliance to the increasing volumes of procedures. Increasingly irritating audits were about all that broke up the boredom. Nothing was ever found to be completely in compliance, and the audit results often disagreed with changes that had been put in place in response to a previous audit. One nuclear safety expert complained in a news article that there were at least six government and independent groups involving hundreds of people hampering the quality of work on safety improvements. "There are too many oversight groups with too many oversight people in them." (Boulder Camera, August 25, 1991)

Heaven help the person that challenged the basis or wisdom of finding any process imperfect. The negative stamp of "resistive to improvement" (bad attitude, in common parlance) was ready to be applied to anyone who dared to ask a question or challenge a directive. The message was clear. The workers would perform a task that generated an audit finding, new procedures would have to be written to prevent or control recurrence, and training would be prepared and given to the workers. Rocky Flats was transitioned away from the production mission, and the value of individual experience and skill was replaced by ritualistic performance and documentation.

Individuals working production lines had the toughest transition. The feelings of pride in personal experience and knowledge were supplanted by frustration with the increasingly intrusive bureaucracy. The pride in what the site had been doing for the national security mission was replaced by the recognition that we were only working for job security. We weren't expected to build anything except reams of bureaucratic paperwork.

The oppressive atmosphere weighed on everyone, including me. I was pleased to see a posting for a management position in the environmental organization, and   I considered whether I should sign it. One component of my consideration was the increased emphasis on environmental compliance. The Resource Conservation and Recovery Act (RCRA) had been signed into law in 1976, but DOE had insisted it did not apply to their sites because the Atomic Energy Act gave them control over regulating the radioactive materials being processed. The courts eventually ruled that DOE had to comply with RCRA after they had successfully irritated the EPA and States. A Compliance Agreement was signed in 1986.   That agreement also included the Comprehensive Environmental Assessment and Response Program, which regulated the process to characterize and clean up contaminated areas.

My first exposure to the Compliance Agreement involved accommodating subcontractors investigating our research activities to identify RCRA regulated wastes. We used wipes wet with solvents to decontaminate working surfaces in our daily work. Of course we treated the used wipes as plutonium-contaminated waste. The use of the solvents, however, made them hazardous waste in addition to being radioactive waste, and the wipes were therefore subject to RCRA regulations.

There was scoffing about why storage and treatment that prevented release of plutonium wouldn't be good enough for traces of solvent that hadn't evaporated while the wipes were being used. The answer was "Because that's the law. It's not because of any improvement to the way the waste is managed."

The Compliance Agreement had very tight schedules that didn't give adequate time to accurately investigate and document all the waste streams at a place as large and complicated as Rocky Flats. As a result, the people doing the waste stream characterization in 1986 had to rush their work, and the final report was filled with errors. Those errors resulted in the survey being part of the basis for the eventual search warrant that alleged illegal environmental activities. (United States District Court (Warrant), June 6, 1989, page 73)

I might have rethought whether I really wanted to have the redundant title of Manager of Environmental Management if I had known federal agents were investigating allegations of environmental crimes at Rocky Flats and were carefully watching a variety of activities, including those RCRA surveys. However, I didn't know about the investigation. I only knew that environmental compliance was gaining increasing emphasis, and I thought that would be a better career than the dead end of production support. My recollection of the impeccable ethics and talent of the environmental people was also a strong positive in my decision to apply for the environmental management job. I signed the posting, and sat through the interviews. Lucky me, I was selected for the position, received the offer, and accepted.

The environmental group had grown since my departure several years earlier, but the mission had changed very little. The management position I accepted was responsible for monitoring air, water, and soil, and reporting the results. I settled into the new job fairly quickly, and enjoyed the professionalism and dedication of the people in the organization. I also enjoyed that there weren't secrets to protect or safes to lock every night. Everything we did was unclassified and reported completely to DOE, Colorado, EPA, and local cities and citizens. Everything possible was done to maintain full compliance with regulations and directives.

I was greeted in my new job with news that there had been exceedences of National Pollutant Discharge Elimination System permit limits for biochemical oxygen demand and fecal coliform for discharges from the sewage treatment plant. These kinds of exceedences were and are common for any sewage treatment plant regardless of whether it was at Rocky Flats or at a similar city sewage treatment plant. Regardless, we began an investigation into why the treatment of wastes from the plant's toilets and showers wasn't working optimally. It became obvious that cold, wet weather had prevented efficient drying and removal of old sludge from the sewage treatment plant. It is an unglamorous fact that new bacteria digest human waste better than old bacteria. I was told by the sewage treatment plant operators that they had requested funding to improve sludge drying, but that the DOE hadn't approved the request. I doubt anyone complained much about that, since DOE owned the facility and the discharge permit.

Presentations were made to DOE and regulatory reports were prepared for them to sign and send to the EPA in compliance with their discharge permit. I didn't hear whether the EPA expressed concern about

46

the report to DOE. I will speculate the team of agents secretly investigating the site cared little about these "garden variety" permit exceedances, although they were eventually mentioned in the search warrant.

My professional life in the months before the raid was going well, or so I thought. The technical experts performing the various assignments of the environmental management organization were capable and prone to question every detail of monitoring results. I was comfortable these talented professionals were doing everything required, and most often insisted that we work beyond the requirements of the regulations.

Then two bad things happened. First, we received reports that cardboard containers of "pondcrete" stored on the 903 pad were slumping and leaking. This material had been removed from the solar evaporation ponds, and was mixed with what was supposed to be enough concrete to make it into a solid block. We later learned there hadn't been enough concrete added, and the supposedly solid blocks became soggy "pond sludge." Operations people set up pumps to collect water from the pad where the material was stored during rain or snow to prevent runoff into the plant ditches. Sometimes there would be too much runoff for the pumps and tankers to keep up.

Massive attention was given to this problem. Briefings were given to DOE managers and the regulators. I recall pondcrete was a regular subject at the Resource Conservation and Recovery Act (RCRA) meetings that were held each Thursday morning in the Building 11 meeting room. DOE people routinely were at those meetings, but usually only listened and seldom ever commented. They would occasionally ask a question.

Briefings were prepared and presented at public meetings and regulatory reports were filed. I was involved in efforts to assure rain or melting snow on the pad was collected to the maximum extent possible. Our organization also collected samples of runoff, had them analyzed, and reported the results. In retrospect, the Justice Department must have judged this to be a fortuitous problem, since the resultant negative publicity came while they were marshalling their justification for a raid. The problem also became part of the plea bargain agreement and the more than eighteen million dollar fine Rockwell would eventually agree to pay.

The second problem, which I judged to be worse, involved a spill of chromic acid, which is a very toxic and corrosive chemical. A researcher in one of the "cold side" (non-nuclear) production buildings noticed the liquid in a chromic acid plating tank was below the required level. A water feed line was turned on to refill the tank, and the worker went home without turning the water off. Sometime during the night the overflowing tank was discovered and the water was turned off. No reports of a spill were filed, because it was believed the overflow had been retained in the building basement. No one knew at that time that the material had seeped to the footing drains and was making its way to the sewage treatment plant.

My wife and I were on vacation in California when the sewage treatment plant called the environmental people to report "something greenish that looks like guacamole from the cafeteria or antifreeze from the garage" entering the system. Analytical people took samples and worked for several days until they finally identified the contaminant. The toxic hexavalent chrome had killed off a good portion of the bacteria in the sewage treatment plant and some of the chrome had reached the holding ponds by the time I returned to the site.

Notifications were made to everyone in upper management within Rockwell and DOE as well as to the local communities, the State, and EPA. Everyone judged this to be a serious problem. A detailed investigation was performed, documented, and distributed. Exhaustive sampling and analysis by onsite and multiple offsite laboratories found trace levels of chrome less than the Safe Drinking Water limits in holding ponds. Approval was received to pump the water into a ditch leading to a pond on Jefferson County Airport property, thereby routing it around Great Western Reservoir. The people responsible for the airport pond seemed happy. They had been concerned about the low water level, and were worried about the bass and blue gill populations.

I would later come to believe it was a stroke of good luck I was gone when the chromic acid spill happened. Perhaps it was paranoia created by the raid, but I suspected it might have made me a target of the Justice Department if I had been there. It probably would have been more difficult to assign accountability against someone who was temporarily filling in, and was not a part of Rocky Flats management. Actions taken after the spill became part of the eventual plea bargain.

Chapter 13

The Secret Investigation of Rocky Flats

or

Some Investigators Wanted to Become Famous

The FBI agent who would eventually be the lead for the investigation of Rocky Flats met with an Assistant U.S. Attorney in June 1988, and is reported to have said, "Let's do Rocky Flats" (Los Angeles Times Magazine, August 8, 1993, page 12). People have described this agent as having a nearly religious belief that bad things were happening at Rocky Flats, and that belief doesn't appear to have changed over the years. It isn't difficult to understand why he was adamant in June 1988 that they should "do Rocky Flats." DOE had been in a lengthy legal argument with the Environmental Protection Agency (EPA) that the Resource Conservation and Recovery Act (RCRA) did not apply to DOE sites, arguing that they had the sole authority to govern their facilities under the Atomic Energy Act. They lost that argument, and later lost other arguments that hazardous materials mixed with radioactive contamination and "residues" containing hazardous materials weren't covered by RCRA. The legal arguments were complicated and could fill books. It wasn't complicated that DOE had made many enemies in the environmental regulatory community who were now eager to see DOE fully comply with the regulations they enforced. One aspect of DOE that wasn't going to change was their fondness for writing about their own deficiencies. This provided FBI agents and Assistant U.S. Attorneys reports from DOE critical of DOE environmental compliance. In May 1987 an EPA investigator from the Office of Criminal Investigation (OCI) was showing the FBI agent and the Assistant U.S. Attorney an internal DOE memo that stated Rocky Flats was "in poor condition generally in terms of environmental compliance, that its permit applications were grossly deficient, and some of its waste facilities were 'patently illegal'."(Los Angeles Times Magazine, August 8, 1993, page 15 and United States District Court (Warrant), June 6, 1989, page 11) Self-criticism had successfully brought additional funding in many previous cases, and perhaps this memo was simply a ploy to get more money. I doubt the purpose was to attract the attention of criminal investigators. There was another DOE memo dated November 13, 1987 from the Manager of DOE's Albuquerque Operations Office, the office that oversaw Rocky Flats operations at that time, which probably gave the investigators even more resolve to proceed. The memo advised "...that DOE should resist the efforts of environmental and public health authorities trying to clean

49

up Rocky Flats and other DOE facilities." It was "… suggested that DOE send a message to EPA that DOE and its management contractors are willing to 'go to the mat' in opposing enforcement actions at DOE facilities" (United States District Court (Warrant), June 6, 1989, pages 56-57)

The investigators were getting closer to a decision to "do Rocky Flats" after "…interviews with two former Rocky Flats employees and the EPA Region 8 regulator…" (United States District Court (Warrant), June 6, 1989, page 9) added to their growing belief that serious crimes were being committed.

We at Rocky Flats, or maybe I should just speak for myself, were not aware what was going on in the offices of the FBI, EPA, and Justice Department. We didn't guess even when we went to look at a water-sampling pump discovered after some employees had reported seeing "a weird thing" next to the culvert carrying Walnut Creek away from Rocky Flats under Indiana Street. We wondered why the pump was covered with camouflage netting, because anyone was welcome to collect samples at that location. Someone speculated that perhaps sample pumps installed by the cities or State had been vandalized, so they had covered the new pump with camouflage net so vandals wouldn't see it from the road. I don't recall anyone speculating the netting was there because the pump was part of a secret investigation. We probably would have frowned in contemplation if we had heard there was a secret investigation, but would have probably shrugged without much concern. Why should we be concerned? Colorado, the cities, and we constantly monitored the water, and there was seldom anything found that would cause concern. We might even have chuckled about the camouflage netting, and said something such as, "that's too feeble an attempt, if the intent was to keep those of us who sample here frequently from noticing it."

We would later learn that samples collected November 15 and 16 1988 were found to contain traces of "mysterious" organic chemicals. The investigators undoubtedly interpreted the results to mean there were illegal discharges of wastes. The EPA Region 8 Toxicologist told investigators on January 3, 1989 "…the combination of chemicals…strongly suggests that the contamination is medical waste originating from a research laboratory or a pharmacy." It was probably of even more interest that the toxicologist said, "One of the chemicals…has been experimentally tested concerning its ability to protect against radiation-induced cellular damage." (United States District Court (Warrant), June 6, 1989, page 98)

The decision to raid Rocky Flats was probably a forgone conclusion by the time the agents found what they believed to be more "smoking guns" late in 1988. They had concluded the 71 and 76 incinerators were operating illegally. I will speculate the investigators decided illegal incineration must be how Rocky Flats was dealing with the court decisions about RCRA-regulated wastes and the limits on amounts of those wastes that could be stored. They were probably unaware that management had taken comprehensive actions that resulted in a significant reduction of wastes generated. Regardless, they set out to confirm what they believed. A spy plane equipped with infrared detection devices recorded temperature of the 71 exhaust stack during night over-flights. They gathered data that they interpreted to be consistent with the incinerator operating and raising the temperature of air exiting the stack. The search warrant states, "...surveillance on the nights of December 9, 10 and 15 indicate that the incinerator was probably being operated on each of those nights." The spy plane also saw a heat trace that indicated water being discharged to Woman Creek on those same dates. (United States District Court (Warrant), June 6, 1989, pages 83 and 99) Seeing those results may have led the investigators to say, "Let's do Rocky Flats."

The Justice Department filed an Application and Affidavit for Search Warrant with the United States District Court of Colorado. The Search Warrant was granted on June 6, 1989, and was assigned Case Number 89-730M. Allegations in the document included illegal treatment, storage and disposal of hazardous and mixed wastes, illegal treatment of hazardous and mixed wastes in an unpermitted incinerator, illegal discharge of pollutants, and false statements and concealment (United States District Court (Warrant), June 6, 1989, pages 11-15). The court sealed the Search Warrant, but of course the allegations that Rocky Flats was doing midnight burning and discharging toxic chemicals to waterways leading to public drinking water supplies became known to the national media shortly after the raid that was authorized by the warrant began.

I've wondered about the timing of the raid. The investigators began their investigation on or about May 1987. They believed they had built a strong case of environmental crimes by late 1988 when they found what they thought was proof that toxic chemicals were being dumped into water supplies and hazardous wastes were being illegally burned. It's my understanding that environmental laws are supposed to protect the environment and the people residing in it. The FBI, EPA, and Justice Department waited nearly half a year before they took action. Why did they allow what they believed to be dangerous practices to continue for so long? Couldn't they have arranged a much quicker raid to end the threats they thought existed? They seem to have believed they were going to easily walk onto the site, observe criminal activities, and haul numerous people away in handcuffs. Where could the allegedly illegally stored waste have been hidden if there was no place to ship it? How could holding tanks, pumps, and pipes involved in the allegedly illegal waste discharges have been hidden? However, the raid wasn't going to be quick, small, or quiet. The raid reportedly made the Governor of Colorado very angry. "I am outraged by the possibility that some possible criminal act has occurred at Rocky Flats that may have endangered the population of this area." (Denver Post, June 7, 1989, page 1A) I wonder whether the Governor knew at that time that the investigation had been going on for over a year and the final evidence had been gathered about half a year earlier. I'm guessing the investigators took their time to organize a large raid with lots of people to gain maximum publicity. I hope I'm wrong, because waiting to gain better publicity wouldn't be a good substitute for protecting people who lived near Rocky Flats. The good news is that it didn't make any difference, because the investigators didn't find the dangerous practices alleged in the search warrant. They managed to scare a bunch of Rocky Flats workers and people who lived near the site, but there was no basis for the fright they caused.

Don't interpret that I'm saying there should not have been a raid. The EPA person assigned to the site and former employees were telling investigators there were illegal and dangerous conditions. DOE had been entangled with EPA in a long-running argument about how waste at all DOE sites was to be managed. DOE had angered the Governor of Idaho by announcing delays in opening the Waste Isolation Pilot Project in New Mexico, the site where it was intended that some waste was to be disposed. That Governor reacted and added difficulty to an already complicated waste management issue by prohibiting continuation of waste shipments from Rocky Flats into his state. (Rocky Mountain News, June 11, 1989, page 48) In addition, there were memos and reports from DOE using words such as "illegal" and the physical evidence that had been collected. It would seem logical that there should have been a raid, and it is also logical it should have happened much sooner.

Perhaps there could have been an earlier raid with less publicity, and that would have given the advantage that the investigators could have just quietly driven back to their offices to console one another when they found none of the things they expected. That would have left the large number of Q-cleared Drug Enforcement Agents (DEA) to stay where they were to enforce drug laws instead of being on temporary assignment it Colorado. That would have saved the inconvenience and eventual anger about the outcome for the 23 citizens who were later randomly selected to sit on a Grand Jury for more than two years. But that certainly is not what happened. Perhaps it would take years of experience as an attorney in the Justice Department to be able to understand why careful preparation for a large, well-publicized raid was more important than stopping what were believed to be dangerous activities.

I can't help but wonder how anyone who worked in Rockwell corporate offices at the time of the raid would feel about the memo from the DOE official saying DOE and its management contractors were willing to "go to the mat" in opposing enforcement actions at DOE facilities. DOE established the policies, decided on levels of funding, gave the directions, and walked away unscathed by what followed. It would have been a violation of federal law for Rockwell to spend their own money to manage problems DOE decided not to fund. They could only legally do the things DOE directed and funded. All Rockwell was allowed to do was to be left alone on the mat. They eventually had to enter criminal guilty pleas to protect innocent employees and save the reputations of the investigators. But I'm getting ahead of myself.

Chapter 14

The FBI Raid Named Operation Desert Glow
or
How to Frighten People

There were reports the agents wanted to bust through the gates at Rocky Flats to initiate the raid. Sort of like Elliot Ness and his team driving through the illegal distillery warehouse doors. Smashing gates guarded by a protective force with automatic weapons and the right to use deadly force was a really bad idea, and arrangements were made for about 80 agents to enter the site secretly and peacefully.

The raid was peaceful, but it didn't remain secret very long. News reports began quickly that a horde of federal agents had commenced a raid at the "super secret Rocky Flats nuclear weapons site because of criminal activities." I was directed to report to a meeting with ten other Rockwell Rocky Flats managers and two serious people in dark suits. The agents stated in general terms that the site was under investigation for criminal environmental activities. The fact that no specific information was given made the meeting feel even more intimidating.

Many of the first news reports focused on interviews with local citizens. Some samples of what they said are:

"It certainly woke everyone up around here."

"I don't want to be out of a life, and I don't want my kids to be out of a life."

"I'm going to sit back and wait...all they're doing is crying wolf at this point."

"I'd never had a sick day in my life before I moved here."

"I feel nuclear weapons are needed, but I don't think my life should be endangered because of it." (Rocky Mountain News, June 18, 1989a, page 21)

I was scared, but it wasn't about the dangers of what we were doing. The unknown about what was going to happen to me the next day was very frightening. It was a sleepless night. My thoughts switched back and forth between questions about what possibly could be the basis for the raid to whether other people were frightened. My answer to the first question was that I could not think of anything that would have caused the raid. My answer to the second question was that of course people would be frightened. Everyone knew Rocky Flats processed very dangerous stuff, and now the government was saying the place wasn't controlling those dangerous materials.

I reported to my office the next morning, tired and quite concerned. Two federal agents arrived, showed me their badges, and told me I would be given one chance to cooperate by admitting details of illegal environmental activities. I told them I'd be glad to cooperate, and would answer any of their questions, but had no idea why they were there. The two agents stood up, announced they would be back, and informed me I would regret not being more helpful. One of them made a point of adjusting the handcuffs on his belt as they left my office.

I remember sitting in my office for quite some time, stunned and worried. I then remembered an army officer class in which the instructor had discussed that anyone can be a leader when everything is going well; it is when frightening things happen that leaders step forward. I didn't know whether I was a real leader or not, but decided I needed to do something. I began to walk around the office areas to gather people for a meeting. The meeting was subdued, and I recall no one spoke other than me. I talked for a while about what I knew, and admitted that wasn't much. I discussed how terrible I felt, and that I imagined all of them felt at least as much anxiety. I also attempted to reassure them, telling them that my opinion was that we were all dedicated professionals working hard to comply with all the laws without compromise. I asked them to look deep within themselves and reconfirm their own professionalism before they got too down on themselves.

I learned later at least one of the frightened people privately approached the investigators and offered to help. I certainly don't blame them for doing this. These people were working to support themselves and their families, and I won't criticize any of them for doing what they thought was necessary for their own protection.

Media coverage was extensive and predictable. One of our more persistent critics was quoted as saying Rocky Flats had made Denver "America's Chernobyl." (Denver Post, June 22, 1989, page 3B) A member of the Governor's Rocky Flats Environmental Monitoring Council said in an article titled, "FBI: Flats burned waste secretly," "We are talking about activities that deserve jail sentences." (Rocky Mountain News, June 10, 1989, page 3b).

The two agents who had done my initial brief interrogation returned the next day, but they didn't begin with threatening statements. One of them asked me to explain environmental programs at Rocky Flats. I responded that would take quite some time, and they assured me they could stay as long as required. I began describing everything I could think of about environmental monitoring. Samples were collected of effluent and ambient air, water, soil, vegetation, and occasionally, wildlife, and detailed reports about the results were widely distributed. The descriptions I gave reinforced to me that we had a very comprehensive environmental program.

I recall thinking the two agents appeared to know very little about Rocky Flats. I considered this to be a ruse, but, if it was, they were very good at hiding their knowledge. When I mentioned that effluent air was sampled from all production operations, including those where the metal beryllium was processed and machined, the agents wanted to know "what's beryllium?" They seemed keenly interested when I explained beryllium to be a toxic, non-radioactive metal that probably caused more health problems for workers than plutonium. The meeting terminated near the end of the day, and I realized I was even more baffled about the raid.

I developed a pattern of taking long walks in the evenings after that first day and in days to follow to deal with my emotions. My anger will occasionally spill over into a verbal outburst, and I would then be thankful for the relative privacy of the path along the irrigation canal behind our home. I would console myself that irrational thoughts were understandable. The Justice Department representing my country wanted to put me in prison, and had dozens of investigators working to achieve that objective. I had always considered myself to be a completely loyal citizen, and had taken an oath when I was commissioned as an Army officer that included a promise to obey the laws of the land. I never considered that oath to have expired. I had been willing to serve in whatever mission I was assigned. Now the country was treating me as if I could not be trusted. George Orwell, who fought against Franco's Fascists in the Spanish Civil War and later wrote the anti-Stalinist books "1984" and "Animal Farm," observed, "People sleep peacefully in their beds at night knowing there are rough men ready to do violence on their behalf." I would have left out the word "rough," but knew in my heart there was something wrong with the amount of distrust I was being accorded by people who had been and continued to be able to sleep peacefully.

The next days and weeks (stretching into months and years) continued to be traumatic. My personal emotions ranged from anxiety, fear, frustration, confusion, and anger. The anger increased as I began to catch up on the news reports and read statements that people at the Rocky Flats plant should be jailed. I noted the local newspapers had even enlisted sports writers to add to the long list of negative stories. An article titled, "Rocky Flatheads," by one sports writer had many observations undoubtedly intended to be clever, such as, "Idi Amin had more credibility than this bunch at DOE, or is that DOA?" (Denver Post, June 8, 1989, page 7B)

I had plenty of time to think, because day after day I was required to sit at a desk outside my office while two agents searched every scrap of paper in every desk drawer and filing cabinet of my office. One of the agents would occasionally direct me to come into the office so they could ask me about a report or note they had extracted from my files. None of the documents or interrogations gave me a clue whether they were searching for anything specific.

It's too bad I hadn't kept myself busy by reading newspapers, because reports were being issued with explanations about the raid. Pressure from the Governor of Colorado and the media had forced the search warrant to be unsealed, and the first report was about "concealed illegal disposal of hazardous and radioactive waste, faked paperwork…and… (discharges of exotic) pollutants into streams…" (Rocky Mountain News, June 9, 1989, page 6) The media had much interest in the list of exotic pollutants, and had begun to report that the pollutants weren't dangerous in just a few days. I hadn't read any of that information when the two agents interrogated me on the subject. One of them asked me to explain Rocky Flats medical operations. I explained there was a fully staffed medical department, and that the Fire Department provided 24 hour a day ambulance service. Sick, injured, or contaminated people received first aid treatment for minor injuries and decontamination as required. People were transported to area hospitals if necessary.

One of the agents interrupted me to tell me they weren't asking about medical treatments. They wanted to know about medical wastes. I told them people who had received offsite radiation therapy were required to collect urine and feces while on site to keep it out of the sanitary sewer system. Workers were welcome to eliminate their personal waste into sewers in their cities, but at Rocky Flats the material had to be treated as process waste because of strict control applied to material going into the sewers.

The agents were becoming agitated. One of them left and returned with a printed page that included a list of chemicals with odd names. They asked whether I had ever heard of any of the compounds. I did recognize one compound, and searched my bookshelf for my copy of "The Condensed Chemical Dictionary." This action attracted intense observation from the agents. I flipped through the book to the page describing the compound and read to them that it was a commonly used in food processing and was naturally produced by decay of vegetation. This information seemed to stir strong emotions in the agent who always seemed to walk into my office in a way that allowed a view of the holstered revolver. He snatched the paper from my hands and waved it at me. "How do you explain the presence of these chemicals in water leaving Rocky Flats?"

"Analytical error?" I responded.

"This isn't a mistake, and it isn't an error! This place has been doing illegal things, and we're going to stay until we find proof. That's when people like you are going to be really sorry."

The "bad cop" then walked quickly out of the office followed by the older agent, the one who always played the "good cop" role. I thought the second agent looked quite perplexed.

The media knew before me that the list of chemicals I had been shown was not the result of analytical error. One of the chemicals had been reported in an article titled "Genetic-test chemical suspected in dumping" to have been used experimentally by the U.S. Military in experiments to reduce the genetic effects caused by radiation. (Denver Post, June 13, 1989, page 2B) But then articles describing the chemicals as innocuous began to appear. One with the title "No exotic chemicals found so far in Flats water," quoted a chemist with the State health department saying, "What I've found so far doesn't indicate a problem..." An epidemiologist said, "Little is known about the exotic chemicals. They don't appear to be terribly toxic..." (Rocky Mountain News, June 15, 1989a, page 31)

Several days passed, and I continued to puzzle over what the agents were seeking, and I wasn't the only one puzzled. Some of the people in the raid would later take jobs at Rocky Flats, and some confided they knew within a day or less the evidence leading to the raid had been misinterpreted. I was also told a water expert at EPA told the agents they should expect to find traces of organic chemicals below a sewage treatment plant. He said he told the FBI that the compounds found at the plant boundary are in foods and medicines, and it should be expected that they would be found in the water leaving any sewage treatment plant. He said he also told them they should ask someone who knows something before they asked for search warrants in the future.

The agent who had become upset with me had been correct when he told me the detection of the chemicals wasn't the result of analytical error. However, the chemicals weren't in the water because of illegal dumping from experimentation on people. The chemicals were there because people pooped and peed in toilets at Rocky Flats after consuming foods and medicines, just like the EPA official had told the investigators. People at Rocky Flats also washed off fragrances and other personal care products when they showered. Treatment of the sewage didn't remove all traces of those foods, medicines, and personal care products at Rocky Flats or at any municipal system. It is unlikely the people who organized the raid on Rocky Flats would want to hear that samples from the Westminster, Broomfield, Denver, Limon, or Deer Trail sewage treatment plants would have revealed a similar list of chemicals. No one had given the Justice Department tips about illegal activities at the municipal sewage treatment plants, so samples weren't collected there.

A headline appeared 12 days after the raid, "Exotic waste identified," and the investigators must have felt things unraveling. "Those 'exotic' chemicals' FBI agents detected in Rocky Flats creeks in November have turned out to be flavoring, fragrances and a compound in common garden vegetables…One of the 14 chemicals was identified as a close relative of…radioprotective agent recently isolated in a family of common vegetables, including broccoli and Brussels sprouts." (Rocky Mountain News, June 18, 1989a, page 7) An article published several years later titled "Chemicals blemish Colorado's water," concluded that the urban Front Range is "especially affected" by chemicals such as those found by investigators at Rocky Flats. (Rocky Mountain News, January 2005, page 4A)

The agents found nothing to justify the raid, and word began to spread about a general degeneration in demeanor of the some of the dozens of agents. Complaints began to surface about overly aggressive, angry, and sometimes threatening actions by agents. Rocky Flats employees began to speak out about the raid. One worker made the insightful comment, "We fear they'll find a technicality to make us red-faced." (Rocky Mountain News, June 25, 1989, page 25)

"My" two agents visited me again with questions about how discharges were managed and reported. I told them preparations for discharge began before the lower holding ponds in the three Rocky Flats drainages began to fill with water. The State of Colorado and cities were contacted in compliance with an "Agreement in Principle," which had been in effect in one form or another since the early 1970s. Water samples were collected and divided with the agencies. The results of analyzing the samples were reviewed, and if the agencies agreed, we opened the valves. Samples were collected of the released water and provided to all the agencies and the Rocky Flats laboratories.

The agents looked very perplexed. One finally asked, "Are discharges ever made because there are high winds?"

I was astonished. "What difference would the wind make? The water would still flow downstream regardless of how hard the wind is blowing."

I later heard the agents had received a tip Rocky Flats was disposing "unwanted plutonium" by burning it and sending it up the stacks during high winds. An article describing the allegations titled "Link between Flats' burns, winds probed," was probably published after I misinterpreted what the agents were asking. (The Denver Post, June 26, 1989, page 1A) The agents were undoubtedly surprised at my answers. I felt foolish when I realized the agents were asking about discharges to the air and not from the ponds. They should have felt foolish to have given any credibility to allegations of "unwanted plutonium" being burned and intentionally discharged up stacks. I continue to find it incredible there were or are people who actually believed we at Rocky Flats would intentionally scatter plutonium over the homes where we lived with our families. Even if someone would believe that, why would anyone believe something so unique and easy to identify could be disposed without detection? The cities, State of Colorado, and EPA all operated sampling programs, and the samples they collected were analyzed by very sensitive techniques.

Another interesting story is about the evidence collected by spy planes with heat detection equipment. The agents believed the plant was doing midnight burning of waste in the 71 incinerator. The heat detectors on the plane showed temperature increases in the effluent air coming from 71 during the night. The agents had expected to find evidence confirming tips about midnight operation of the incinerator, so they concluded the heat increase was being caused by waste being burned. The building heating system was later conjectured to be the cause of these temperature increases.   Anyone living in Colorado for even a short time learns the temperatures drop quickly after the sun goes down in December. Thermostats register the drop in temperature and turn on the heating systems. A spy plane flying over a Colorado home when the furnace turns on after sundown would also find evidence of "midnight burning."

I can't answer questions about what the plane saw from other buildings. The investigators had believed the incinerator in Building 76 was also likely to be operating illegally, but I haven't seen any discussion of any building other than 71. People hearing about the 71 incinerator after the raid probably imagined a sizable plume of exhaust. The headlines about illegal operations would have created that impression. However, this particular incinerator was inside a glove box, and would have fit inside a 55-gallon drum. It was used to burn small quantities of plutonium-contaminated paper and plastic. I have heard of no evidence that the incinerator was operating when it wasn't supposed to be, and I've heard nothing about the investigators finding any evidence to the contrary.

The Los Angeles Times magazine reported that the prosecutor on the investigation team had an EPA expert analyze the infrared data collected by the spy plane. The expert told him he couldn't say the heat spikes from the 71 stacks weren't from the building heating system. He also said the heat traces that had been interpreted as discharges into the creeks might have been runoff. The article concluded, "In truth, the prosecutor's case just then had started to unravel." (Los Angeles Times Magazine, August 8, 1993, page 18)

I've read that one of the agents involved in the Rocky Flats raid and at least some of the members of the Grand Jury remain convinced there was midnight burning in the 71 incinerator. One rumor circulated at Rocky Flats was that agents had interrogated a sizable number of the more than 300 people who worked in 71, and that only two were invited to testify about the incinerator to the Grand Jury. The rumor was that those were the only two people who said "yes" or "maybe" to whether there had been midnight burning. If that rumor was true, the Grand Jury heard from none of the more than 300 people who said "no" or "I doubt it." I wish there were a way to verify this, but the proceedings of the Grand Jury are sealed. I will speculate that the rumor was true. Why else would the people who sat on the jury continue to be convinced about the truth of the allegations if they had heard the full body of evidence?

I provided a link in the online version of this book to the infrared video taken by the Justice Department that convinced them the incinerator was operating at night in Building 771. Unfortunately, the link is no longer active. A blog posting asking for an active link hasn't yet found a response.

Chapter 15

The Raid Continues
or
Rocky Flats Verifies It Has No Friends

The length of the raid seemed to be interminable, and some of the events I witnessed or heard about remain baffling to me. One day an excited person rushed up to me and described that a crowd of agents had assembled on the top of 44, the building where uranium and beryllium were processed and machined. The agents had lined up at one end of the roof an arm length from each other, and walked very slowly to the other end. They appeared to be studying every inch of the roof with intense scrutiny. The only explanation I can conceive is they had received a tip that the building had a "secret vent." The allegation of "secret vents" had been kicked around among the site critics for years. Regardless of that speculation, I'm certain the agents didn't find anything except vents documented in routine environmental reports. Experts assembled by the State of Colorado to study the site in the early 1990s reported no "secret" or "unreported" vents were found.

As an aside, I observed that anyone who investigated Rocky Flats and found no new evidence was always immediately lumped into the "part of the conspiracy" category. So the experts who couldn't find any "secret" or "unreported" vents undoubtedly were considered to have been part of the cover up.

There was intense distrust of Rocky Flats generated by the raid, to understate the obvious. Government officials who had been routinely informed by verbal and written reports of monitoring at and around the site must have been quite confused. Their agencies had been doing independent monitoring for decades, and, with the exception of the tritium incident in 1973, nothing had been found that hadn't been previously reported by Rocky Flats. One of those confused people, I'm speculating, was the head of what was then called the Colorado Department of Health. He had told the Colorado Water Quality Control Commission the week before the raid that Rocky Flats' operations weren't causing any risks. He told them after the raid that new events made those statements inappropriate.

My opinion is that few of the elected officials in office at the time of the raid did the right thing. Those who announced that people at Rocky Flats should be jailed without trial should have been removed from office. Those who pressured the Justice Department to reveal the basis of the raid to address understandable public concern should be commended. The

Governor of Colorado at that time led those who did what was right by applying pressure to force the Justice Department to address increasing public concerns.

I really didn't comprehend the extent of the public's concern about the raid and what was being investigated until a Rocky Flats co-worker from a research and development organization waved me down one day as I was walking to a meeting. This person and I had worked closely together for a number of years, and I believed we had each other's mutual trust and respect. I was surprised, even a bit shocked, when the person asked, "What in the world have you people done? It's awful. My family and friends are asking why I work for such a terrible place. They know I'm an honest, law-abiding citizen, but I don't think they believe me when I tell them I don't know what caused this raid."

I responded with a long explanation that I was becoming convinced the raid was a mistake, and the allegations of criminal activity would be dismissed.

"Nonsense! Do you think I'm stupid? Elliot Ness doesn't show up with a hundred agents unless something really terrible is going on."

I've mentally replayed that conversation many times. I'm certain that Rocky Flats worker wasn't the only one with those thoughts.

The one time I was given the opportunity to discuss the fear created by the raid with the Justice Department agents was during what I would learn was the last time the usual two agents visited my office. The one who always played the good cop asked me whether there was any information I wanted to share with them (perhaps fishing for a reason for the raid).

"Sure. We've worked here for decades to honestly share information with our communities. This raid has destroyed those years of diligent effort by honest, dedicated, loyal people." (I didn't add anything such as "unwarranted, inappropriate, and misdirected" in front of the word "raid," but I wish I had.)

The two agents were silent, and the good cop appeared to be intently studying the floor, before responding, "If things are as you believe them to be, then that is what we will find at the end." Then they left, and I never saw either of them again.

One outcome of the raid was the complete change of mission. We had previously transitioned from a production facility to a safety compliance mission. We now transitioned to a copying factory. Document subpoenas required that records of all kinds be turned over to investigators, and the decision was made that copies had to be retained. Draft and final reports, logbooks, laboratory records, computer hard drives and disks, typewriter tapes, calendars with hand written notes, etc., etc., etc., had to be copied and provided to the federal investigators. Additional copy machines were brought in and began to run continuously, or as continuously as they could be made to work. Literally millions of pages of copies were made and shipped to the Justice Department in hundreds of boxes.

The document searching effort did uncover one interesting document in my files. I mentioned previously there were two agents who did a complete search of all files in my office. One of the agents summoned me into the office. I was greeted with what I later realized was a friendly smile.

"I thought you might want this. It was stuck into one of your files."

I was handed a 4X10 certificate. It was a gift certificate to the LaBelles department store (which has been out of business for years). The five-dollar gift certificates had been given to all Rocky Flats Employees to commemorate achievement of a Health and Safety milestone, such as a million hours of work without a lost time injury.

I told the agent thanks, and they left for what I would learn was the final time. I felt I had been given an apology in the only manner they could invent.

In retrospect the decision to raid Rocky Flats is easy to understand. Negative reports by DOE established that Rocky Flats wasn't to be trusted. Who isn't going to believe a report when the owner of a facility publicizes criticism of operations for which they are responsible? Critics who disagreed with the mission of Rocky Flats were understandably also concerned about the reports. The atmosphere of suspicion festered for years until some Justice Department agents were given tips about alleged illegal activities. These tips originated, in my opinion, mostly from people who had little direct knowledge of what was happening at the site. Many of those people were opposed to anything to do with the manufacture of nuclear weapons. Some probably thought that people willing to build parts for bombs would be willing to ignore laws. People who thought that way didn't know us very well. Most people who worked at Rocky Flats had to have a security clearance, and clearance wouldn't be awarded to anyone who wasn't a law-abiding U.S. citizen. That indisputable fact apparently made no impression on the Justice Department.

One of the tips is said to have originated with a regulator who chose not to have the security background check required to obtain a clearance. That choice prevented the regulator from being able to view classified information and operations. This regulator, who made no effort to hide anti-Rocky Flats opinions, told people he had been blindfolded during tours of certain Rocky Flats facilities. I have heard the regulator told fellow critics of Rocky Flats the blindfold was used to prevent him from seeing illegal waste disposal operations. I've read references to this event in several documents, including in the search warrant (United States District Court (Warrant), June 6, 1989, page 63). I know the areas where the blindfold was applied, and there were no waste disposal operations, legal or illegal. There were, however, things an uncleared person was not allowed to see.

The regulator was interviewed by a local paper a few years later, and the article describing the interview was on an inside page. The gist of the reported statements was something like, "Evidently the things we thought were going on, weren't. That doesn't matter, because good came of this. The place is shut down, as it should be." I think it was a different interview when this person was quoted as saying, "I'm giddy at the thought of closing Rocky Flats." This person apparently didn't believe facts were important. This is a sample of what happens when the attitude is that the end result is all that matters. The "giddy" comment isn't the most memorable one made by the critics when interviewed after the raid. There was one person who said hearing of the raid was as good as a three-orgasm night. I haven't yet located the article where this statement was quoted, but I'm still looking.

Perhaps the biggest surprise to me about the raid and aftermath was yet to come. I expected the Justice Department to announce that the tips and misinterpreted physical evidence had led them to conduct a raid, but they hadn't found anything they believed they would find. The raid with dozens of agents, combing through millions of pages of documents revealed virtually nothing that hadn't been formally and publicly reported prior to the raid. So, no harm, no foul? Not quite. The Justice Department wasn't finished. The investigation continued for years. The raid and events that followed resulted in spending untold amounts of taxpayer money. Consider, for example, the number of DOE employees at Rocky Flats as one small measure of the financial impact of the raid. There had been about 20 AEC people at the Flats when I first began as a Dow employee. This number grew to hundreds of DOE employees and their direct report subcontractors doing "oversight" of a place that produced nothing after the raid. It was a taxpayer's nightmare, and a bureaucrat's dream come true.

Chapter 16

Herbicides in the Water!
Herbicides in the Water!
or
Transforming a Molehill into a Mountain

The Governor of Colorado was pressuring every agency that had any involvement with the raid and the continuing investigation to identify whether neighbors of Rocky Flats were at risk. He also asked the Colorado Water Quality Control Commission to establish the most restrictive discharge water quality standards possible for Rocky Flats. The Commission complied by holding hearings as the first step in establishing strict discharge limits. One of the Commissioners asked a witness at one of these hearings why Rocky Flats had been selected as the site to build plutonium components for nuclear weapons. "Why would anyone build such a place just upstream of municipal drinking water supplies?" In fact, the Atomic Energy Commission studied more than 30 possible locations, and they selected Rocky Flats in part because it was isolated from nearby cities at that time. There also were not any drinking water supply reservoirs below the site until much later. The downstream municipalities decided to convert both Great Western Reservoir and Standley Lake from agricultural supply to drinking water supply several years after Rocky Flats began production operations. (ChemRisk Tasks 3 & 4, August 1992, pages 181 and 184) Furthermore, the cities had dug a ditch below Rocky Flats around Great Western Reservoir after the raid, so it wasn't an issue any more. (Denver Post, June 13, 1989)

It was obvious the Commission knew what it was going to do before the hearings started. They pulled together a nationwide list of all existing and proposed drinking water quality standards and used the strictest of those standards to establish limits for the waterways where Rocky Flats water had to be discharged. The Commission also calculated limits for plutonium, uranium, americium and tritium based on the years of data reported by Rocky Flats. The sum of their efforts resulted in well over two hundred parameters that required sampling and analysis before a Rocky Flats pond could be drained. Fortunately for us, the water in Rocky Flats ponds was more pure that most drinking water.

Not that we didn't have problems. The increased water management requirements for Rocky Flats resulted in installation of all manner of pipes and pumps at the ponds. One day I received a report that a diesel pump at one of the ponds had leaked, and there was a small area of pond water that had a "visible sheen" from about a cup of diesel fuel that made into the pond. The term "visible sheen" required that the US Coast Guard be notified there had been a spill of petroleum products into "waters of the United States." I called the national spill response center, and the Coast Guard official on the line was quite confused.

"Tell me where you are again."

"The Rocky Flats plant near Golden, Colorado."

"And what water is being threatened."

"The water in a pond on the Walnut Creek drainage,"

"How much petroleum product is involved?"

"One estimate is there was about a cup spilled."

"And why are you calling me?"

"Because the law requires me to report this to you."

Put yourself in the position of that Coast Guard officer. This was the same office where reports were received after the spill off the coast of Alaska by the Exxon Valdez.

DOE became nervous about questions the investigators were asking about spraying water from sewage treatment plant discharges on the hillsides, and directed us to end all spraying operations. That change resulted in the need to manage more water. The spraying was started in the 1970s when everyone's goal was to discharge as little water from Rocky Flats as possible. The treated water was collected in a holding pond and then sprayed onto nearby areas. There were some dry years when most if not all water from the Rocky Flats sewage treatment plant evaporated after being sprayed. The water discharge permit issued by the EPA had language requiring spraying the water "in accordance with good engineering practice." There had been internal battles over the propriety of the spraying operations since before I began my management position in the Environmental Management group. Many believed the spraying should be terminated when the ground was saturated or when the temperatures dropped below freezing, and I initially was on that side of the argument. Spraying in cold weather had caused blocks of ice to form around the pipes each winter, and the workers driving into the east gate named the area "Icehenge." I don't know whether the regulators who drove past the area gave it the same name, but the ice blocks were clearly visible to anyone entering the East gate.

My opinion about the spraying operations began to change the more I studied both sides of the argument. The goal was to evaporate every possible drop of water. Spraying until the ground was saturated and runoff began made certain that was being achieved. A ditch had been put in below the spray field to collect runoff and drain it to the holding ponds.

That would allow further management of the water. Spraying allowed significant evaporation and additional treatment would occur from the interaction of runoff water with dirt, plants, and sunlight. The book, "The Ambushed Grand Jury" (McKinley and Balkany) would charge that the spraying operations had resulted in contamination, but the Director of CDPHE dismissed the allegations based on sampling and analysis of the areas involved.

I advocated the advantages of spraying, but DOE disagreed, directed all spray operations were to cease, and cease they did. DOE owned the plant, they were the ones who had signed the discharge permit, and we operated at their direction. Water once evaporated by spraying began to accumulate in the ponds along with precipitation runoff. Ponds began to fill, and samples were collected and divided with the local communities, State, and EPA. The Rocky Flats portion of the samples were delivered to contract laboratories to be analyzed for the extensive list of parameters for which drinking water standards had been established by the Colorado Water Quality Control Commission. The plutonium, uranium, americium, and tritium levels were less than the new standards. The water passed the drinking water purity requirements for over two hundred parameters. Traces of herbicides called atrazine and simazine were found that did exceed the limits.

Rocky Flats did use herbicides. Security people thought it would be a bad idea to have weeds that might make a good hiding place around the perimeter of the production areas. So the areas were sprayed by a licensed contractor to kill the weeds and prevent new ones. I attended a meeting between DOE and one of the cities after the results had been confirmed. One of the city officials told the DOE, "You people are so stupid. If you were dogs, we'd have to teach you to bark. How could you be so stupid to get atrazine in your water?"

I would have left the meeting if I had been alone, but it wasn't my meeting. I was there, as usual, as an observer, and wasn't allowed to participate unless directed by DOE. The DOE people stayed "for further discussions." Mostly what we heard was that we couldn't release the water from the pond unless we first removed the herbicides.

I learned the city that accused the DOE of stupidity also used atrazine for weed control in their parks and open spaces. Atrazine is widely used by most cities and other governmental agencies for the same purpose, but the largest use is agricultural weed control. It is found in most surface water. U.S. Geologic Survey analysis of water samples collected in the South Platte Basin (the basin where the pond would be discharged) reported atrazine is found in most samples (Capel and Larsen, 2001 and Rocky Mountain News, January 20, 2005).

Regardless of the fact the water would be discharged to streams and rivers that contained atrazine, we were directed to treat the water before it could be released. Within a couple of weeks we had an activated carbon system purchased with a large amount of taxpayer money, delivered, and installed.

There was a meeting in the offices of one of the local cities the week after treating and draining the water from the pond. I don't recall the date, but it must have been in late summer or early fall of 1989. I remember there were representatives of Rocky Flats, the State of Colorado, and one of the cities at the meeting. The early part of the meeting was unremarkable, unless you would consider the information in the large stacks of papers on the table to be remarkable. The reports listed analytical data from samples of the discharged water that showed the discharged water had been pure enough to meet all of the most restrictive discharge limits in the world. There did seem to be a conflict between the State of Colorado representative and the city representative. Suddenly and surprisingly, the person from the city burst out in a quite loud voice, "You don't get it! The last thing we wanted was for the water to meet all the limits. We wanted the Commission to set all these limits, because no one could ever imagine that any water would meet all of them. Now we're going to have to figure out a new approach."

The Colorado representative looked quite startled, and asked, "What do you mean?"

"I mean the water wasn't going to be in a drinking water supply. Do you think anyone really cared about water quality? We just wanted the Commission to give us political leverage."

The color had now almost completely left the face of the Colorado representative. "You mean you used the Commission for politics?"

The meeting quickly broke up as the people from the city and State left to have private discussions. The full meeting reassembled just long enough to allow an announcement the meeting was over.

I don't claim to understand the politics that were being applied at the time I've described, but I did know water purity was unimportant. It was only important that the water was "politically contaminated."

Chapter 17

Aftermath of the Raid
or
That Sound is Hundreds of Millions of Dollars Being Sucked Into Rocky Flats

DOE tossed Rockwell aside as quickly as they could after the raid and awarded EG&G a multimillion dollar contract to manage Rocky Flats. Rockwell attempted after its departure to defend itself and its employees from the allegations originating from the raid, and even took full page ads in local papers to present the message that Rockwell was and always had been a law-abiding company, and that its employees were good people who were doing their best to operate Rocky Flats properly, safely, and within the law (Rockwell, January 1990). Local papers had editorials with scathing responses. The Denver Post version said, "Instead of taking your lumps and skedaddling as any other discredited contractor might have done, your company bowed out of Rocky Flats this week by smugly proclaiming complete innocence. Most galling was your suggestion that your critics might have been motivated by 'political expediency' rather than real interest in the welfare of...people who work at the plant...and ...who live in the metro area adjoining it. Yours is a company, after all, that let scores of serious safety problems go uncorrected..."

"It may be that you have been unjustly pilloried for violating anti-pollution laws after the FBI raid...--an action that appears to have been based in part on an ill-founded allegation...But it's irresponsible to imply that you should be held blameless."

"Coloradoans understand...that some of the accusations lodged against you during the FBI raid were unwarranted. But they also understand that your management at Rocky Flats was woefully insufficient...."

"Your attempt to entirely whitewash your record only further diminishes what little credibility lingered after your hasty departure." (Denver Post, January 4, 2000)

DOE also publicly criticized Rockwell, saying they "were fed up with Rockwell's recent behavior" in the announcement that EG&G was going to be the new contractor. DOE agreed to pay EG&G 2.5 billion to operate Rocky Flats for four years. Rockwell would have been paid the same amount to operate the plant for five years. EG&G also was given $15 million up front, and could earn another $10 million a year in performance fees. (Denver Post, October 12, 1989, page 9A) It was interesting that this happened very quickly compared to the usual lengthy competitive procurement process required for much smaller contracts. Negotiations were done secretly, or at least I didn't know anything about them.

EG&G came to the site with direction from DOE to spare no expense in environmental matters. A new, larger environmental organization was announced that would have several high-level management positions. One of the positions posted had the title Clean Water Act Division Manager. The newspapers were full of stories discussing that one prime driver for the raid was violations of the Clean Water Act, and it was clear to everyone the investigations were still active. I asked an attorney whether there would be any "personal exposure" (a term I had recently learned), if I applied. The advice given was that there wouldn't be any change to my personal risk. I would already be held responsible if there had been illegal discharges I knew about or should have known about. The advice wasn't very reassuring. However, I didn't know of any illegal discharges, and our extensive investigations since the raid hadn't found anything new. I tried to take reassurance from that and signed the posting.

A meeting was held between the personnel department and the new EG&G management team to discuss candidates for the new positions. All but one of the positions had several candidates. Apparently only one person had signed the posting for the Clean Water Act Division Manager, and that person happened to be me. My preference is to claim I was selected for the position because of my superior qualifications, although that would be the one time in this book that I would claim something I know not to be true. I was selected for the position that gained the widely renamed title of "designated felon" because I was the only person who applied.

History has shown that I didn't become the designated felon, and there were positives about the position. My new job not only gave me a significant increase in salary, it also gave me a chance to hire people who had outstanding credentials. My plan was to hire people smarter than me, give them direction about what I needed them to do, and leave them alone except to ask for status reports if they didn't volunteer the information. My new management peers and I had approvals to hire several dozen environmental professionals to staff our organizations. A few slots were filled with people from the previous environmental organizations, but a major recruiting effort was launched for dozens of new people. One of the other new managers who had recently arrived from off site announced at a staff meeting that there would be no one hired from existing Rocky Flats people, "since there was no way to tell who might have taken part in the illegal activity." I wondered what the illegal activities might have been, and, after consulting with the managers reporting to me, decided to hire a mix of new people and existing people from the Rocky Flats technical ranks. This, in my opinion, was one of my more brilliant decisions. Many of the young professional engineers and scientists at the site recognized opportunities were being created by growth in the environmental groups, and my group was about the only place they could find an entry. We had our pick from many outstanding people. We assembled a talented group of people, with about half being new to the site and the other half being current employees who had proven themselves to be superior performers. There was an advantage to having this mix. People in other organizations needed some help in the basics when they were given an assignment.

I was approached by a frustrated new employee from one of the other groups with the inquiry, "I've been told to evaluate the air emission monitoring system in Building 771. Where is that building, how do I get there and who can I talk to that would know about the system?"

The people we hired from the existing technical staff knew the site well enough to know how the find the buildings and also knew the people to talk to. They also didn't approach operating people as if they were criminals. It isn't surprising our group usually had more cooperation from operational people.

I'm certain the Justice Department also was celebrating the opportunities being presented by the sudden growth in Rocky Flats environmental operations. The raid hadn't turned up the desired "smoking gun" evidence, but I'm certain the investigators believed some of the many new environmental professionals at the site would turn up something. It's possible they could even have some of their own people apply, be hired, and work under cover.

I made requests at our staff meetings that I be informed if anyone found anything illegal. The following is a close approximation of what I said in more than one meeting. "I'm aware some of you new folks wanted to come here to find the things that are being done incorrectly, and to stop those things. That's great; we all want to stop anything not being done legally or properly. I do request you tell me of anything you find at the same time you tell the Justice Department. I can go to jail if there are illegal things going on I should have known about. We interviewed and hired all of you because of your professional qualifications and personal qualities. I hope you believe that gives me the right to the professional courtesy of telling me what you are doing and anything you might find that would cause a risk of me going to jail. Yes, this is very serious business, and I want all of you out there on the site to find anything there is to be found. Our job is to comply with laws, and I expect nothing but perfection in that assignment."

At least a couple of field investigations performed by new people did attract the attention of Justice Department agents. One investigation resulted in a report from a consultant observing there weren't any algae in the last large holding pond on the north drainage. The biologist's judgment was that the water must contain something toxic to algae. I was told the consultant was visited by a federal agent asking for details. Multiple samples were collected from the pond and analyzed by every conceivable method. Nothing was found that could explain why algae wouldn't grow in the water. One morning a young biologist arrived in my office, smiling broadly.

"I know pond A-4 doesn't have algae."

"Why?"

"There's no food."

"I'm not following."

"Algae need nutrients. Algae need food just like anything else, and there isn't any in the pond water. The water is too clean to support algae."

"That sounds great, but do you know for certain?"

"I thought the pond looked crystal clear, which might mean it is crystal pure water. So I spiked a sample with some traces of phosphate, and there was an overnight algae bloom. If the goal is to have algae growing in the pond, throw in some phosphate."

I was relieved and appreciative. I imagined there was disappointment at the Justice Department.

Another day a different young scientist walked into my office.

"This place put something toxic into pond C-2 last spring. "

"What was it?"

"I don't know yet, but I'll find out. It would be in your best interest if you helped me find out what it was."

"Why do you think this?"

"There are fish of all maturities in the other ponds, but nothing more than a few months old in C-2. Something toxic killed all the fish in pond C-2 on or about the month of May."

I opened my desk drawer and began thumbing through files. I extracted a file, put it on the desk, and quickly found what I wanted.

"Pond C-2 was discharged to completely dry in May. That would certainly kill the fish that didn't leave with the water. Your interpretation that something killed the fish in May is correct, but it was lack of water that killed the fish. You can copy these records if you wish. These are the records of plans to do the discharge, sampling and analysis results showing the water quality was acceptable for discharge, records of notifying the cities and the State, their concurrences, volume of water discharged, and results of sampling and analyzing the discharges. Please just return the originals to me after you make copies. And thank you for sharing your concerns with me. I realize you probably didn't have to do that, and I appreciate it."

Evidently the scientist decided that copies of the file weren't needed, and I've never seen that person again.

The large numbers of new people didn't find anything illegal, or at least I never heard of anything illegal being found. I would enjoy seeing the massive records kept by the agents as they watched and listened to what we were doing. I would particularly enjoy seeing the notes about a telephone conversation I was having with a friend who happened to work for the site as an environmental consultant. We discussed business matters, and then I said, "By the way, to the agent listening to this call, I'm going to talk about some social plans for a bit. You undoubtedly will continue to record our conversation, but I just thought I'd give you the chance to take a break if you wish."

My friend later advised me, "You really shouldn't tug on Superman's cape."

I was very impressed by the group of people I worked with, but there was a constant cloud of suspicion from the on-going investigation. I became quite worried about what I thought was the generally depressing work atmosphere. I became sufficiently concerned about morale to arrange a private meeting with the manager of the Employee Assistance Program (EAP) to talk about whether I was exaggerating the problem. That person was skeptical my visit was really about employee morale and not a personal problem.

"We frequently have a person come here to tell us they know someone who has a problem. It usually takes considerable assurance they can safely tell us they are the one with a substance abuse problem and there is a guarantee of no risk to their employment if they self-report it and follow our program to address it."

I assured the person the subject of the visit, morale, was legitimate, and I wanted to know whether my concerns were real or imagined.

"You're probably underestimating the problem. I've never seen nor heard about a place as bad as this. People have no positive feedback here, except for a routine paycheck and good benefits. People once apparently had pride in what was made here and that they always met schedules with high quality work. It is difficult or impossible to be proud when nothing is being produced. The constant hammering that they don't have the skill to do anything well or the desire to do anything safely doesn't help. They get this message constantly, and when they aren't being lectured about their deficiencies they spend most of their time in the cafeteria playing cards. Then they go home and see headlines about criminal activities going on here. Their family and neighbors ask them how they can work in such a terrible place. Does that answer why morale is low?"

I asked what I could do to help the people in my organization.

"Lay them off. You wouldn't believe the number of people we see who say that's what they want. They can't justify quitting, because they know they can't replace the pay and benefits they get here."

I wasn't certain what to do, but I called a meeting, did the best I could at telling the people what I had heard, and passed out EAP pamphlets. Perhaps that wasn't as lame as I feared. I began to have requests for private meetings where I heard some incredibly personal stories. I usually responded with what I hoped were encouraging words. I would confirm that I understood the level of difficulty. Our only choice was to support each other, and to always continue to work diligently and professionally. And I reinforced that we could never forget to always do the right thing. "Do the right thing," is a simple homily that is often difficult to apply. Sometimes doing the right thing has immediate negative consequences. Immediately reporting the occasional unusual result from monitoring always attracted a storm of questions and criticisms. However, we always made the reports because we knew that it was right to do so.

It wasn't long after my meeting with the manager of EAP that an internal memo from that person to the director of the occupational health department was given to the media. A sampling from the memo that was published in the newspaper includes:

"Employee morale has taken a nosedive..."

"...sweeping changes have had an intense impact on employees and the problems are causing employees severe stress at home and on the job."

"...workers attitudes pose potential safety problems."

"Employees are getting mixed messages to restore the plant to safe operating condition and to complete work quickly..."

"There exists an overall distrust of management and a generalized belief the company is self-serving and deceitful." (Denver Post, October 24, 1990, page 3B)

I continue to have residual anger for what happened at Rocky Flats and the damage that was done to the people who worked there. DOE started the negative slide with its destructive criticism process and insistence that procedures were more important than individual skill. The Justice Department injected the toxicity of fear, doubt, and shame. Then

DOE jettisoned Rockwell for doing what DOE had directed them to do. Why wouldn't morale take a dive?

Chapter 18

The Grand Jury

or

The Search for Why There Was a Raid

Anyone reading this expecting to learn specifics about the Grand Jury investigation of Rocky Flats will be disappointed. Proceedings from that investigation are secret by law. What follows is information taken from various published accounts and my observations and speculations.

A special Grand Jury was assembled to consider evidence of environmental crimes at Rocky Flats. In July 1989 about 50 people had postcards in their mail summoning them to the federal courthouse in Denver. Twenty-three people were selected by random drawing to sit on the jury (Los Angeles Times Magazine, August 8, 1993, page 16). The first Colorado special grand jury of all time was empanelled in August 1989 (United States Attorney Statement, September 23, 1992, page 5). The judge instructed the 23 people they were to consider whether or not illegal activity had been occurring at Rocky Flats. They were to consider the information being gathered by the dozens of agents and included in the millions of pages of documentation obtained by subpoena and to hear testimony from 100 or so people. They could recommend indictments if they believed the evidence warranted, and they could write a report on issues that did not lead to indictments. (Wolpe, January 4, 1993, pages 121-123) The jury met numerous times over more than two years. At the end some of the members wanted to issue indictments, but, according to news reports, the Justice Department didn't believe they had found sufficient evidence to justify indictments. Some members of the Grand Jury wanted people to go to prison, but the Justice Department, with the exception of at least one person, was satisfied with a plea bargain in which Rockwell pled guilty to felonies and paid millions of dollars in fines. This angered some of the Grand Jury members, and someone allegedly illegally released at least some information about their investigation to a newspaper. Some voiced their disappointment by accusing the Justice Department of a cover up. The coauthor of the book, "The Ambushed Grand Jury" explained why the raid was part of the cover up in a Hustler magazine article (not a source I would normally use, but it was in the Rocky Flats Reading Room). The article, titled "Rocky Mountain Meltdown," quoted the coauthor as saying, "...it seems to us the purpose of the FBI raid was to cover up what the DOE did rather than actually prosecute it. It was really a sham raid." When asked, "How exactly does a phony raid help in a cover up more so than a traditional veil of government silence, secrecy and denial? Wouldn't not responding have been a better approach?" The answer given was that citizens groups, "…namely the Sierra Club had started filing lawsuits. They were going to be able to request all sorts of documents that would have shown a lot of what was going on. I believe the purpose of the raid in large part was to take control of that documentation…." (David and Cromer, November 2004)

I find that reasoning astonishing. If a raid with about 80 federal agents lasting two weeks or so and issuing subpoenas for millions of pages of documents followed by two years of Grand Jury hearings is a sham or a phony raid, I'd hate to see a real one! I know my organization copied everything that went to the investigators, and that was the policy for the entire site. Documents provided in response to one subpoena therefore would have been available for response to another subpoena. It is my understanding that only the actual Grand Jury proceedings were sealed. I would have bought it if it had been said they found a government bureaucracy that had created problems and refused to take responsibility for their own actions. I would have not only bought that, I would have endorsed it.

I have thought about why there was a raid and why, despite the fact the agents didn't find what they expected, there was a Grand Jury empanelled. To understand why there was a raid it is first necessary to consider the depth of suspicion of the place that led critics to expect there were laws being broken. The Rocky Flats production mission was to produce parts for nuclear weapons, and many people believed then and still believe that mission was immoral. The secrecy required to protect information about classified production activities created suspicion about everything. DOE angered many when it insisted that environmental laws didn't apply to their facilities. DOE managers went so far as to write memos saying they and their contractors should fight the regulators. There were people working at the plant talking about how dangerous and unsafe the work was, and DOE released reports criticizing safety of operations. All of this reinforced the suspicions of people who passionately believed bad things were going on behind the "wall of secrecy." Cap all that by the numerous incriminating self-critical reports issued by DOE. Then the Justice Department received results from water sampling and thermal data from spy plane flights that seemed to confirm the suspicions. It is understandable that one of the members of the investigative team then said, "Let's do Rocky Flats!"

Unfortunately for the planners, the raid wasn't the expected immediate success. The agents hadn't found the "smoking gun evidence" at the end of the first day, first week, first month, or first year. Now what should they do? Not to worry, Rocky Flats was a huge, complicated place. All manner of dangerous and toxic materials were used in operations too numerous to imagine, and the processing buildings and other areas were contaminated with those dangerous and toxic materials. The Justice Department decided not to do the right thing and announce the raid had not found the expected evidence of illegal activities. They decided to continue to investigate and have a Grand Jury empanelled. They did succeed at painting such a negative picture to the Grand Jury that they lost control of at least some members.

A review of Rockwell's plea bargain by Rockwell easily reveals the fines they paid were not for the sensational items in the search warrant. It was based on reports prepared by Rockwell, submitted to DOE, and sent by them to the regulators before the raid. Those reports and all the other environmental reports were available for the Justice Department in the offices of the various regulatory agencies before the raid, and did not require the raid or the subpoenas that followed for discovery.

A relatively small part of the fines, if $300,000 can be considered small, was for sewage treatment plant discharges that exceeded permit limits for fecal coliform and biochemical oxygen demand. Rockwell was forced to plead guilty to three counts of "Negligent Violation of CWA Permit Conditions" for exceeding Biochemical Oxygen Demand (BOD) and fecal coliform limits, and agreed to pay the $300,000. (U.S. District Court (Plea) March 26, 1992b, page 3). This information was gathered from reports prepared by Rockwell, delivered to DOE, and then sent by DOE to the EPA as required by the water discharge permit that had been issued to DOE.

Violations of water discharge permits are treated very differently by the State of Colorado by comparison with what happened with Rocky Flats. The Denver Post published an article in a Sunday Paper in December 2004 on the subject. There is a table listing the number of pollution-discharge limits for the 25 most frequent violators. There were 2161 violations and the total of all fines was $123,190 compared to the three counts that Rockwell pled guilty to and was fined $300,000. Six of the 25 violators listed in the Denver Post article had fines levied, and those were all municipal sewage treatment plants. There were 19 "frequent violators" that had no fines levied. There was one industrial permit holder, a coal-bed methane producer, that had 251 violations, and had no fines levied. There was one Superfund mine cleanup site that had 59 violations, and had no fines levied (Denver Post, December19, 2004, pages 1A, 16A-18A).

How far did the Justice Department have to stretch to find a reason for the Rocky Flats raid? They had to find a way to get Rockwell to agree to a criminal plea bargain. They had the Grand Jury eager to issue indictments, and they used that to extract a settlement from Rockwell.

Chapter 19

Aftermath of the Grand Jury

or

A Strange Ambush

News reports have said at least some members of the Rocky Flats Grand Jury want the proceeding of their investigations to be made public, but the courts mostly have held fast to the laws that keep grand jury deliberations secret. Someone familiar with the Grand Jury apparently did reveal some of the proceedings to at least one newspaper. I imagine there are people in the legal community who would appreciate the opportunity to make the acquaintance of that person.

People have said to me, "I bet you live in fear that the things the Grand Jury heard will some day be opened to outside investigation." I predict many if not most readers will be confounded to hear I would have no fear if that were to happen, and that I don't criticize the Rocky Flats Grand Jury members who were and are frustrated that their work did not result in indictments of individuals. They performed their civic duty by giving up a considerable amount of their time and energy to investigate what was going on at Rocky Flats. What I advocate is an in-depth investigation of why those people retain their belief that indictments were appropriate and necessary while the dominant belief in the Justice Department was that full presentation of the evidence would prove there was nothing illegal that occurred. Logic indicates the Justice Department presented only the information to the Grand Jury that painted the picture they wanted. It is well known that grand jury testimony is often one-sided, and those under investigation have no rights to submit a defense. The anger expressed by Grand Jury members is based on what they were told and shown, and that anger is undoubtedly completely legitimate. I also am convinced that the Grand Jury anger would be redirected if they were able to see all the evidence collected by the investigators, and not just the evidence that was selected to save face for the Justice Department.

Many of the attorneys on the prosecution team who saw all of the evidence made statements that support the accuracy of what I wrote in the previous paragraph. The Congressional committee that subpoenaed four members of the prosecution team issued a report that was very critical of the failure to indict individuals, and I suggest you get yourself a copy of the Wolpe Report if you want to check what I'm saying. The committee observed, "Individual members of the grand jury have... made allegations of misconduct by the U.S. Attorney." (Wolpe, January 4, 1993, pages 16-17) Buried within the report is information that describes the

81

level of disagreement between the attorneys. The Deputy Assistant Attorney General from the Environment and Natural Resources Division, who was a key member of the investigation's legal team, testified, *"Virtually none of the allegations contained in the search warrant were borne out after a full investigation.* For example, the most celebrated allegation—that of midnight burning of hazardous wastes—was based on aerial infrared monitoring of the site. As it turned out, the monitoring equipment was defective... If the level of the fine and number of guilty pleas are an appropriate measure, I can assure you the result we have reached by plea agreement is considerably better than what we could have expected had we indicted the company and various individuals, and gone to trial. There were no 'high level' officials involved who had sufficient knowledge to be charged and convicted of knowing violations. Additionally, the company had some quite persuasive defenses to many of the corporate charges to which they are nonetheless are pleading guilty. Quite frankly, although we can meet standards under the Principles of Federal Prosecution, *had we known at the time of the warrant what we know now, it is likely this matter would have been resolved civilly. That is primarily because of the marginal evidence of criminal intentional misconduct, and the lack of any significant environmental harm."* (Emphasis added) (Wolpe, January 3, 1993, page 30)

Of the three other principal Justice Department attorneys on the case, the U.S. Attorney, Colorado, also "...maintained that there was not sufficient evidence to indict individuals." The Trial attorney from the Environmental Crimes Section and the Assistant U.S. Attorney, Colorado apparently were "somewhat more positive" (about the possibility of having indictments that would hold up). In sworn testimony they "...tried to avoid any inference that individual indictments were given up for the plea bargain." The U.S. Attorney further said, *"We have to be careful what we say to avoid an allegation that we are holding individuals hostage."* (Emphasis added) (Wolpe, January 3, 1993, page 42)

There are further statements quite interesting to consider if you are one of those who just can't believe Rocky Flats wasn't guilty of environmental crimes, especially since Rockwell pled guilty to criminal environmental crimes. An Assistant U.S. Attorney, Colorado that worked at least briefly on the Rocky Flats case apparently worked on it long enough to develop strong opinions. There was testimony that this Attorney told the FBI agent that the case against Rockwell was "...a series of no-harm technical permit-type violations ordinarily the sort which would be handled administratively and for which criminal prosecution of Rockwell might be 'marginally justified' overstates the matter... *the case against Rockwell 'should probably be declined' and was 'worth nothing'."* (Emphasis added) Yet another Trial Attorney with the Environmental Crimes Section who worked on the case from March 1990 to April 1991 was quoted in testimony that "...*but for the search warrant this matter would have been handled civilly...believed the case against Rockwell to be 'marginal'...and 'if it had been up to him, he would decline the whole thing'."* (Emphasis added) (United States District Court (Limine), November 10, 1997, page 20) This same attorney was quoted in a Justice Department report with a statement I hope is the one thing people who read this will remember. The attorney *"...suggested that as far as individual culpability is concerned, he was unsure whether there was a single person at Rockwell who did not believe he was in good faith subjectively attempting to comply with the environmental laws."* (Emphasis added) (United States District Court (Limine), November 10, 1997, page 24)

Why was there such a gap between what the Grand Jury thought and the comments under oath by the members of the Justice Department legal team? Some members of the Grand Jury were or are angry that individuals from DOE and Rockwell weren't indicted. However, most of the lawyers who saw all the evidence did not believe indictments should be issued, or, if they were issued, that they would stand up in court. Why would this be? I will speculate the answer is buried in the mundane statistics comparing what the Grand Jury was shown and told from the total body of evidence. I've read that the investigation resulted in gathering 944 boxes of documents, although I'm surprised that number wasn't higher. There were nearly 800 witness interviews. The Grand Jury heard testimony from about 110 witnesses. (United States District Court (Limine), November 10, 1997 page 17) I mentioned a rumor in a previous chapter that the Justice Department only arranged Grand Jury testimony from the two people from 71 Building who said that the incinerator was or might have been operating. The Grand Jury did not hear testimony from the hundreds of people who said it wasn't operating. There is confirmation that the testimony presented to the Grand Jury was very selective. The lead EPA investigator was interviewed for an article titled, "It's Toast, All the ooze that's fit to print about Rocky Flats." The article said the investigator judged there had not been a conspiracy after saying he read every one of the documents that filled 185 boxes (which would have been only a small amount of the documents). He observed the Grand Jury was only presented with a fraction of that information. (Westword, February 3-9, 2005, page 3)

I believe the only fair method of evaluating the true story is to look at all the evidence. I will speculate that a review of the full story would lead people to agree with the several attorneys on the prosecution team that indictments were not justified, and if they had been issued the people would not have been convicted. The U.S. Attorney wrote "I have even heard it suggested...that our ethical obligation to charge only those for whom a reasonable likelihood of conviction exists should have been sacrificed to the presumed deterrence that may have resulted by charging individuals with criminal offenses, *even though the prosecution of individuals would neither have been fair nor have likely resulted in conviction.*" (Emphasis added) (United States Attorney, September 23, 1992, page 14)

I doubt there will ever be a new investigation of what happened with the Grand Jury. Even accusations that the files collected by the investigators would contain proof of contaminated areas not included in the site cleanup couldn't generate enough interest to have people sift through the files. An article titled, "Rocky Flats info brouhaha," said "Three months after the U.S. Attorney said he would consider allowing Rocky Flats cleanup officials to see secret grand jury records on illegal dumping, no one has asked to review them." The EPA Assistant Regional Manager said he wanted prosecutors' help in narrowing the search. "To go through, page by page, an entire room full of documents probably would take many months...I don't have the time." (Rocky Mountain News, August 20, 2004, page 1) I interpret that to mean revisiting the full body of evidence is not going to happen. However, I predict some Grand Jury members would have second thoughts about their conclusions if they could see all the evidence.

There is one aspect of all my reading about the investigators and their reaction to what they found that continues to baffle me. The lead FBI agent on the investigation (who is no longer with the agency) apparently remains adamant that crimes occurred and there was a conspiracy to cover up the evidence. This person is eager to express anger about the outcome. The beliefs and anger persist despite judgment by numerous attorneys working the case that evidence was not found that could support indictments. Several newspaper articles have been written about this person. One, titled "Servant of the People, Agent of Change," mentions that the Assistant U.S. Attorney, who had been the FBI agent's friend and other Justice Department staff, met with the agent and allegedly told him, "You're not stuck with how you felt before. Even today, your opinion can change." (Boulder Weekly, January 6-13, 2005, page 2) The agent obviously didn't or wouldn't agree.

The fact the Justice Department didn't issue indictments validates for me the EPA investigator who said there was no conspiracy got it right and the FBI agent got it wrong. The Justice Department knew indictments would not stand up to the bright glare of truth from the full evidence, and they decided a different approach was needed to try to salvage their reputations.

Chapter 20

The Plea Bargain
or
Why Did Rockwell Plead Guilty?

Examination of the plea bargain extracted from Rockwell by the Justice Department offers validation the driving force at the end of the investigation was to find some way for the feds to save face. Rockwell charged that the Justice Department resorted to threatening Rockwell employees with indictments. (United States District Court (Limine), November 10, 1997, page 4), and they certainly should have known the facts about those threats. Rockwell wasn't alone in this belief. There is speculation in the book, "The Ambushed Grand Jury" that the Justice Department used the Grand Jury to extract the plea bargain from Rockwell. Grand Jury members thought the presentation of new evidence dried up several months before the end of their service. The prosecutors filled in time by repeating themselves and rereading information that had already been presented. "The prosecution may have been stalling to keep the Grand Jury in session to pressure Rockwell with the possibility of indictment." (The Ambushed Grand Jury, McKinley and Balkany, pages 140-141)

The Justice Department apparently had decided they had to convince Rockwell they would never give up without a guilty plea and fine big enough to prevent Justice Department embarrassment. Those people must have been good poker players, because several of the prosecution team had expressed the opinion there wasn't a sufficient basis for charging individuals that would hold up in trial. However, the magnitude of the raid, the fear created among people living in the area by the sensational allegations, and the lengthy Grand Jury proceedings required a scalp to be taken from Rockwell. Rockwell pled guilty so good people wouldn't have to endure being indicted and convicted in the court of public opinion by their neighbors. The Colorado U.S. Attorney told the Wolpe committee they "did not find...the kind of deceptive conduct we thought may have occurred." A Justice Department report stated, "...there was no evidence ...of concealment or cover-up on the part of any Rockwell employee." The attorney preparing the report also wrote, "...at no time...did any individual come forward to acknowledge or identify serious environmental criminal conduct." (United States District Court (Limine) November 10, 1997, pages 22-23) It would be remarkable to believe there could have been people at the plant who knew of illegal activities and not given the information to the investigators to protect themselves. A statement by the investigators confirmed what Rockwell had said. "It should be noted that, unlike nearly every criminal investigation…at no time did any individual come forward to acknowledge or identify serious criminal conduct or to give useful substantial inculpatory information which could be corroborated about the alleged crimes of others." (United States Attorney, September 23, 1992, page 7)

There was a simple reason the raid and the frightening situation it created did not uncover a conspiracy. I assure you there was no conspiracy to crack, or it would have been cracked it with ease. There were many scared people who would have told all, if there had been anything to tell. I knew at least one of the people who was threatened by the Justice Department, and that good, honest person was terrified. I did not know at the time that the Justice Department had sent letters threatening indictment to several Rockwell employees. (Wolpe, January 4, 1993, page 37) The reason a terribly shaken Rockwell employee came in my office and closed the door to have a private conversation made more sense to me after I learned that. I've often reflected on what was said, and it makes me not at all proud of our Justice Department.

"What am I going to do? They told me they are going to indict me within the next month if I don't come clean with them. I told them I would tell them anything. I asked them what they wanted to hear, and they told me they were the ones doing the questioning. I told them I would even make up stuff and swear to it if that's what they wanted. They told me they were only interested in factual evidence that I had been directed to engage in illegal activities. I asked what the activities were, and they told me they were the ones asking the questions. I don't know what to do."

"Do you really think they would indict you if you haven't broken any laws?"

"Yes, I absolutely believe them. And what would I do? The news would find out in no time. I can hear my neighbors telling reporters how surprised they were to learn that one of the criminals at Rocky Flats lives right next door. They'll say things like, 'Seems like such a nice person; I guess you never really can know.' What will I tell my family? They don't deserve this."

My response was weak and ineffective. I didn't even believe myself when I said I couldn't believe the government would stoop that low.

Five of the people being threatened by the government and Rockwell filed suit against the Justice Department about intimidation with blunt threats. The Denver U.S. Attorney's office agreed to a secret settlement. (Denver Post, April 11, 1991) I hope the person who was in my office that day was part of that action, and that there was a sincere apology from the government, at a minimum.

The Justice Department was struggling with what to do. They weren't finding evidence to justify the raid and all its massive publicity. They had been feeding the Grand Jury all the negative information they could find, and those people were chomping at the bit to indict Rockwell and DOE managers. But then a ray of hope appeared to the investigative team. An Assistant U.S. Attorney in Los Angeles called the Colorado Assistant U.S. Attorney. The conversation was about a case where Rockwell had pled guilty to defrauding the Air Force out of $400,000, and Rockwell had paid a $5 million dollar fine. It was said, "...Rockwell wanted to come to the table and make a plea agreement wherein no individuals would be charged and Rockwell would pay a fine." (United States District Court (Limine), November 10, 1997, page 26) The ray of hope for the Justice Department was that Rockwell would plead guilty and pay large fines to protect its employees.

Unfortunately for the Justice Department, there wasn't universal agreement that Rockwell should plead guilty and pay a fine. One U.S. attorney "...actually said that the government should pay Rockwell." Others were willing to settle for $1-$6 million dollars. (Wolpe, January 4, 1993, page 22) The good news from the perspective of the Justice Department was that their ploy of threatening to ruin the lives of some Rockwell people worked. Rockwell fully understood that indictments associated with the Rocky Flats case would be devastating to individuals. They had taken the position early in the plea bargain negotiations that they were unwilling to plead guilty to environmental crimes, but were "...willing to pay a substantial criminal fine if it could thereby protect its employees from totally unwarranted prosecution." (United States District Court (Limine), November 10, 1997, page 32) They cared enough about their employees that they eventually agreed to pay a fine of $18.5 million; they also agreed to plead guilty to crimes that aren't called crimes anywhere else. The Justice Department bragged about the size of the fines, apparently proving the theory that size matters. "I guess it's a little bit like going to the Olympics or setting a world record, and someone runs the hundred yard dash and they beat the record by a hundredth of a second, and that's a new number. Eighteen and a half million dollars beats the old record by a factor of four times." (United States District Court (Sentencing) June 8, 1992, page 28)

I don't know whether neighbors of Rocky Flats were relieved to hear that the sensational allegations reported by the media shortly after the raid weren't included in the list when Rockwell pled guilty. "From

Rockwell's perspective, there have been some positive aspects to this investigation. Rockwell is gratified that one result of the investigation was to establish that the more significant suspicions and more sensational allegations of wrongdoing originally leveled against Rockwell have been disproven.... It was those allegations of secret and clandestine criminal activity which went to the forefront of the public consciousness at the time the original search warrant was executed." (United States District Court (Sentencing), June 8, 1992, page 7) The U.S. Attorney said, "...there is no indication that the charged conduct...resulted in substantial off-site physiological harm." (United States District Court (Sentencing) June 8, 1992, page 31) The Judge commented, "...the environmental harm caused by the charged violations was generally limited to inside the plant's boundaries." (United States District Court (Sentencing) June 8, 1992, page 40)

I wondered why the words "substantial" and "generally limited" were used in the comments instead of the words "no" and "completely limited" until I found a small section of the Wolpe report that might provide the answers. That report said, "Although the chrome charge ultimately pled to was a CWA misdemeanor, it did include the off-site discharge of chromic acid to the public waterways..." (Wolpe, January 4, 1993, page 68) As I mentioned earlier, the "off-site discharge" of the pond water that contained less than drinking water standard levels of chrome was approved by all regulatory agencies and went to a fishing pond. I will just say that's a pretty small reason to infer there needed to be any hedging in the language. Perhaps the hedging goes back to the "exotic chemicals" found in water discharges. The U. S. Attorney said, "...the specific chemicals noted were present in extremely small amounts and are not believed to have caused any significant risk to the public health or the environment." (United States Attorney, September 23, 1992, page 9) Other sources were quoted as reporting, "Those 'exotic' chemicals FBI agents detected in Rocky Flats water in November have turned out to be flavoring, fragrances, and a compound found in common garden vegetables." (Rocky Mountain News, June 18, 1989, page 7 and United States District Court (Limine) November 10, 1997, page 16) I'll give one more reference to the issue of whether there were off-site discharges. I'll go into the Grand Jury report in more detail in the next chapter, but there is at least one allegation by the Grand Jury and response from the Justice Department in the redacted report that is pertinent to this discussion. The Grand Jury reported that the raid "...discovered...illegal discharges of pollutants, hazardous materials, and radioactive matter into the Platte River, Woman Creek, Walnut Creek, and the drinking water supplies for the Cities of Broomfield and Westminster, Colorado." The Justice Department wrote in reply, "...there is no evidence of any Rocky Flats pollutants...being discharged into the Platte River. *Extremely small amounts of radioactive material have reached Walnut and Woman Creeks over the years, and have sometimes reached Great Western Reservoir and Standley Lake. This has been publicly and widely known by federal, state and local regulators for many years. There is no...evidence that any such materials, during the period investigated, resulted in any criminal violation or any imminent or new (or unknown) health threat."* (Colorado Federal District Court, February 19, 1992, pages 8-10) (Emphasis added)

I think this is a good place to mention that I believe Rockwell was the only "participant" in this entire process that earned my respect. I admire what Rockwell did. The Justice Department didn't announce immediately after the raid they hadn't found what they expected. They expanded the investigation, evidently certain they would find something to justify their raid and all the publicity. The Grand Jury followed the instructions they received by a judge, and I have no complaint about the members of that jury. The Grand Jury was formed and fed negative stories about Rocky Flats while the investigators continued to sift through hundreds of boxes of records. The investigators were able to find only what they had already seen in records filed by the site to Colorado and the EPA. Those records confirmed DOE had angered the regulatory community because they had believed they weren't required to comply with some environmental laws. However, the Justice Department couldn't indict DOE, an agency of the federal government that had statutory immunity. The Justice Department turned to the only solution they had left. They intensified threats to indict Rockwell employees. Rockwell, in my opinion, gave the government a way out while demonstrating loyalty to their people. They agreed to plead guilty to criminal violations of environmental law, violations that are seldom if ever treated as criminal in other circumstances. Rockwell also agreed to pay multi-million dollar fines. Rockwell's actions gave the Justice Department a way out and protected good people from having their lives ruined by the humiliation of being convicted in the court of public opinion.

Rockwell probably reasoned that the plea bargain would be recognized as absurd. A lawyer once told me they test their stories about why a defendant can't be guilty by explaining it to someone in their office. They can use the theory in court if they can get through the explanation without giggling at its absurdity. Rockwell thought enough of its people to agree to a plea bargain that didn't pass a giggle test, and was probably astonished they didn't hear any giggling when the news of the plea bargain was read. They pled guilty to problems reported to regulators and the public before the raid. Most of the problems had been caused by DOE disagreements with the regulatory agencies and/or DOE failing to provide the funds to solve the problems. The problems hadn't resulted in offsite releases or impacts, and I've not heard of the environmental problems included in the plea agreement being called criminal at other facilities.

I'll bet Rockwell is still waiting to hear what they expected to be guffaws of disbelief over the plea bargain. However, instead of recognizing the absurdity of the plea bargain, the news media simply (and I really do mean "simply") focused on Rockwell pleading guilty to criminal environmental crimes. There is no dispute that Rockwell pled guilty to criminal environmental crimes. It is clearly written in legal documents that Rockwell signed the agreement. "On March 26, 1992, Defendant Rockwell International, a corporation, entered a conditional plea of guilty to a ten count Information charging five counts of illegal treatment and storage of hazardous wastes in violation of federal statute and five counts of violation of the Clean Water Act in violation of federal statute." (United States District Court (Sentencing), June 8, 1992, pages 35-36) Two things concerned me about that quote. First, I haven't been able to learn about why "Information" was stuck in there. It is probably some sort of legal term. Also, I was surprised about the words "conditional plea of guilty." There is a clarifying statement on the next page, "The Court finds that Defendant Rockwell did enter an unequivocal plea of guilty on March 26." (United States District Court (Sentencing), June 8, 1992, page 37)

I don't recall any in-depth (or even shallow) analysis of the believability of what was included in the plea bargain when it was announced. There was no comparison to how violations of environmental laws were handled at other DOE sites or other Colorado industrial and municipal dischargers, and no defense of Rockwell from anyone, including me.

Chapter 21

The Grand Jury Anger About Failure to Indict Individuals

or

Why Was Rockwell Alone on the Mat?

The frustration, disappointment, confusion, and anger expressed by the Grand Jury about the outcome of the investigation attracted almost as much attention as the raid. I will warn you that describing the legal maneuvering and the chasm between the Grand Jury and Justice Department was complicated, and I think both of them got it wrong in some cases. Good luck with wading through this chapter. It is complex, but important.

I doubt the Justice Department anticipated the negative responses when they announced the plea bargain. Several members of the Grand Jury began to prepare a report the judge told them was one of their responsibilities when they were given their original instructions. That report presented allegations of crimes not mentioned in the plea agreement and demanded indictment of individuals. The preparation of this report would drive a wedge between the government and the Grand Jury. When the U.S. Attorney heard the jurors were writing a report he advised them not to meet again. Citing their independence, the foreman was less than complimentary in his response. He is reported to have said to his fellow jurors, "If you are going to let one government chickenshit lawyer tell you what to do, you're not part of America." The judge withheld all but clerical assistance to the grand jury as they worked on their report. (Wolpe, January 4, 1993, page 136)

"In September of 1992, some of the members of the special grand jury...provided a Denver newspaper—and subsequently other media—with a draft of their report and a 'presentment' of charges that they drafted as a substitute for the negotiated information presented by the U.S. Attorney. Their charges allegedly named Rockwell managers and DOE officials. Individual members of the grand jury (sic) have also made allegations of misconduct by the U.S. Attorney. It is almost unprecedented for grand jurors to risk criminal contempt of court by violating their official oath of secrecy..." (Wolpe, January 4, 1993, pages 16-17) This tactic, although illegal and therefore risky, apparently succeeded at forcing the government to take note of their report. The outcome was a redacted or edited report. One reason the report was redacted was to remove names of individuals the Grand Jury allegedly believed should be indicted. The discussion of various components of the report given below follows the format of presenting a charge made by the Grand Jury followed by a response by the Justice Department. I've included my disagreements in some cases. My interpretation is that the Grand Jury was primarily angry that DOE wasn't held accountable, and they thought Rocky Flats operations should be terminated. The Introduction of the Grand Jury report taken by itself and the Justice Department response gives a flavor for the broad level of disagreement:

Grand Jury: "The Department of Energy..., its contractors – Rockwell...and many of their respective employees have engaged in an on-going criminal enterprise at the Rocky Flats Plant...which has violated Federal environmental laws. This criminal enterprise continues to operate today..." The report continues, "...and it promises to continue operating (in an unchanged manner) into the future unless our Government, its contractors, and their respective employees are made subject to the law."

"United States' Response: The grand jury's statement is both legally and factually wrong. There is no preponderance of evidence or legal basis for the grand jury to accuse DOE of engaging in an 'on-going criminal enterprise...which violate(s) Federal environmental laws.'" The Justice department interpreted that the Grand Jury wanted DOE to be prosecuted for wastes they thought were being illegally stored. The people writing the Grand Jury report wanted the operations generating the wastes to be ended, or, in other words, they wanted Rocky Flats shut down. The Justice Department wrote, "However, as the grand jury was repeatedly informed, storage of such wastes...are not crimes and are covered by various orders and regulatory agreements." (Colorado Federal District Court, February 19, 1992, pages 2-3)

The Grand Jury report accuses that, "DOE managed the plant with an attitude of indifference toward environmental laws."

"United States' Response: The evidence shows that Rockwell, far more than DOE, actually controlled Rocky Flats on a day-to-day basis..." (Colorado Federal District Court, February 19, 1992, pages 25-26)

I will dispute the Justice Department's response in strong terms, because I can't think of anything that would justify the statement that Rockwell and not DOE was in control of Rocky Flats. It is true that Rockwell performed the day-to-day operations, but the directions came from DOE.

There is another allegation in the Grand Jury report stating, "The sovereign immunity of the Federal Government does not immunize individual government employees from prosecution for their criminal conduct." The gist is that the Grand Jury believed DOE officials should have been indicted. I have strong disagreements with the third paragraph of the response from the Justice Department, which says, "In the areas of the criminal charges – illegal treatment and storage of hazardous mixed wastes, spray irrigation and operation of the sewage treatment plant, DOE was either wholly unaware of the problem, or was not aware of anything approaching the true nature of the problem. It was not until after the search warrant was executed, in June 1989, that the RFAO was finally provided sufficient resources to conduct a reasonable degree of independent oversight." (Colorado Federal District Court, February 19, 1992, pages 51-53) I assure you that DOE was fully informed of problems with operations of the sewage treatment plant and spray irrigation. I know this, because I was involved in briefings to DOE about those operations and problems with them. It sickens me to read that "DOE...was not aware..." because we worked diligently to inform them. We knew they were the owner of the site and thought they were ultimately responsible for the problems. Writing this made it clear to me I and other Rockwell managers were guilty of extreme naivety.

The government continued their outlandish premise that DOE was unaware of environmental problems in numerous legal documents. The Sentencing Memorandum prepared by the Justice Department had many statements that Rockwell failed to inform DOE of problems. It was asserted in that document, "DOE was not aware of the chronic problems with spray irrigation or their magnitude until after the search warrant in June 1989." The prosecutors had documentary evidence showing that statement wasn't true. "The prosecutors obtained from DOE's own files during the June 1989 raid a viewgraph used by Rockwell (prepared by my organization) at a February 1988 presentation concerning spray irrigation, which described the identical spray irrigation problems..." DOJ admitted in a 1994 report about the Rocky Flats criminal investigation that spray irrigation 'was not...an instance where the responsible individuals sought to cover up the problem'." (United States District Court (Limine), November 10, 1997, pages 64-66)

Rockwell and I aren't the only ones to believe DOE was fully aware of what was going on. "Fundamentally, based on the material that was available, it appears as if in one area -- pondcrete/saltcrete -- the prosecutors made erroneous statements about the lack of knowledge on the part of DOE personnel. The prosecutors maintained...DOE personnel were not aware of problems... However ...a September 17, 1987 ...memo...gives a clear indication that DOE knew both the condition of pondcrete/saltcrete and the reasons for it..." (Wolpe, January 4, 1993, page 110)

94

An important part of my job and other environmental managers was to assure that DOE, EPA, CDH, the cities, and anyone else who wanted to know what we were doing or experiencing were informed about problems such as concerns about spray irrigation, pondcrete storage and risk of runoff, the chromic acid spill, etc. We would brief our DOE contacts before we went to offsite meetings with information about issues. I will say with all due respect, which in this instance means there is no respect due, statements such as "DOE was not informed," are absurd.

I want to give at least a brief description of the sentencing memos and the sentencing hearing before I cease and desist with all these details. For those who recall discussions that Rockwell got off easy, the Judge doing the sentencing hearing after the guilty plea said, "To some, a fine of $18.5 million may appear insufficient. That is, however, the maximum fine that the Court can impose for the charges that have been filed, even if the Court were to reject the plea agreement and the defendant should be found guilty on all counts." (United States District Court (Sentencing), June 8, 1992, page 39)

I'm not inclined to make you wade through a discussion of the litany of differences comparing what the plaintiffs and defendants said on each of the ten counts to which Rockwell pled guilty. I'll use the example of pondcrete, which was made by mixing liquid sludge from the solar ponds with Portland cement, to explain the absurdity of the plea agreement. The pondcrete preparation process was needed to meet the requirements of a 1986 Compliance Agreement between DOE and Colorado. Pondcrete was originally classified by DOE as a non-RCRA, low-level radioactive waste, and it was to be shipped to the Nevada Test Site. The shipments had to be stopped to comply with RCRA and the Compliance Agreement when the waste was reclassified as hazardous waste and low-level mixed waste. No RCRA permitted site existed at that time to accept pondcrete for storage or disposal. There was too little cement being added to some blocks (a quality control problem that Rockwell should have managed better), and many of the blocks began to turn into a wet putty and slump. The tri-wall cardboard containers were not designed for storage out of doors, and some began to leak. Anyone looking at the ugly mess that resulted would have been disgusted. The Justice Department charged Rockwell with illegal storage of mixed hazardous wastes. (Plaintiff's Sentencing Memorandum, Pages 28-51)

Rockwell makes the following points about pondcrete:

- The production and packaging methods "…were designed, at the order of DOE and CDH, for short term use only…"

95

- DOE refused "…to accept these waste forms for permanent storage in Nevada because DOE had not obtained the necessary permits for its Nevada site."
- Rockwell requested to stop pondcrete production "…until the storage problems could be solved. CDH refused, and insisted that the original schedule (for making blocks out of solar pond sludge) be maintained."
- Rockwell requested money "…to build weatherproof shelters to protect the waste forms until shipments to Nevada could resume. DOE refused, stating that shipments to the Nevada site would soon resume."
- There was "…never any test which detected any pondcrete constituent at any harmful level in any reservoir or any place off site." (United States District Court (Defendants), March 26, 1992, pages 41-56)

I was fascinated with the Rockwell discussion about the fine included in the plea agreement for failure to file a RCRA permit for storage of pondcrete on the 904 pad until December 1987, although storage began at that location in July 1987. Reading Rockwell's thoughts about what caused that failure to file the required permit provides an insight into where the problems included in the guilty plea really originated. Rockwell agreed that the permit had not been filed on the required date, and wrote, "This statement is correct, and $2,000,000 in fines are to be levied for this offense." Seems pretty straight forward, doesn't it? However, read on. *"What the Plaintiff omits to say is that Rockwell notified DOE in early 1987 that additional storage space would be required beyond the first storage area. DOE advised CDH of this fact and was directed to file a RCRA interim status permit. Rockwell prepared a complete application for storage on Pad 904 for DOE's signature, and on June 9, 1987 delivered it to the DOE office on site at Rocky Flats. Rockwell has no knowledge of what happened thereafter until the application was filed by DOE, apparently six months later."* (Emphasis added) (United States District Court (Defendants), March 26, 1992, pages 54-55)

I will speculate that this is one example why several Justice Department lawyers were concerned indictments of Rockwell managers would not result in conviction. What would you have found if you were sitting on a jury hearing evidence that a Rockwell official should be convicted of failing to file a permit application when you learned it was DOE that was supposed to do the filing, that Rockwell met the schedule for delivering the document to DOE, and that DOE delayed sending it in for six months? I'd be quite surprised that very many people would declare a Rockwell manager guilty after hearing that.

I want to discuss some thoughts about the anger some people on the Grand Jury and the lead FBI investigator have expressed that some DOE officials weren't indicted as a result of their efforts. The prosecutors apparently didn't realize until after their raid that the contract between DOE and Rockwell would probably require DOE to pay any fines levied against Rockwell. The Justice Department found this to be quite disturbing. They knew the government would look ridiculous if millions of dollars and numerous years of prosecutorial resources were devoted to a costly trial only to have any fines reimbursed by DOE. They recognized Congress and the public would be very critical of them. It became apparent that according to contract agreements DOE would pay all the fines unless the lead Rockwell manager at Rocky Flats was convicted of a crime or if Rockwell allowed those fines to be their responsibility in a plea bargain. I will interpret Rockwell demonstrated they would not only protect the living employees, but would also protect the memory of at least one who was deceased. They commented they would not have liabilities unless top contractor officials could be proven to have some connection with criminal behavior, and no such connection could be proven. (United States District Court (Limine), November 10, 1997, page 46) Why do I say Rockwell was protecting the memory of someone with this language? The only person that met the legal definition of a top contractor official could never be convicted of anything; he died after a difficult battle with cancer. Rockwell could have said that, and the legal fact that conviction was impossible would have been indisputable. However, in what I read to be a classy approach, they only said the official couldn't be convicted of criminal behavior.

The prosecutors only had one solution remaining, and they turned up the pressure on Rockwell by threatening to indict its managers. The Justice Department realized there would be little reason to hope DOE would help it avoid looking ridiculous as long as DOE officials remained targets of the investigation. They recognized that "whatever the likelihood that DOE would have been required to reimburse Rockwell, this prospect was so disastrous to the entirety of the prosecution effort that this concession by Rockwell...was critical to the prosecutors." A meeting was arranged between the Justice Department and DOE in late February in 1991. The Colorado Assistant U.S. Attorney said after that meeting that DOE "would take a hard line position in terms of not agreeing to indemnify Rockwell for any fines or penalties resulting from the criminal case." Soon after a DOE official sent a memo that "none of the likely indictees are DOE employees." (United States District Court (Limine), November 10, 1997, pages 46-48) I would interpret that to mean DOE decided not to join Rockwell "on the mat."

The Justice Department got what they wanted from DOE, because DOE agreed they would insist that Rockwell pay all legal fees and fines despite the fact their contract indemnified them from those costs. The U.S. Attorney bragged, "It is important to note this is the first time that DOE has ever not reimbursed an operating contractor..." (United States Attorney, September 23, 1992, page 11)

It was also February 1991 when a DOE person, a talented person I respected, called me, and sounded depressed. The words were something like, "There was just an announcement that no DOE people will be indicted. It's embarrassing. People are celebrating in the halls. We just went though a series of meetings about the importance of teamwork with contractors, and now we're celebrating that DOE will be treated differently than the contractor."

I remembered the end of Orwell's Animal Farm, when the sign was changed to "All Animals Are Equal, But Some Animals are More Equal Than Others." I also recall the DOE official's comments that it was "... suggested that DOE send a message to EPA that DOE and its management contractors are willing to 'go to the mat' in opposing enforcement actions at DOE facilities" (United States District Court (Warrant), June 6, 1989, pages 56-57) I wonder whether Rockwell was surprised to find themselves alone on the mat, or whether they had come to expect equality and teamwork would not apply.

To those who are finding all these details about the legal proceeding tedious, the good news is that I'm about to go back to what was happening at Rocky Flats. For those who want more details, there was once a Rocky Flats Reading Room in the Front Range Library with hundreds of feet of shelves filled with documents about the place, and many of the references I've included at the end of this were housed there. The bad news is that DOE decided to close the doors of the Reading Room and box up all that information. The last report I heard was that it was all going to be delivered to a part of the University of Colorado library, but that making the information available for review there has been delayed because someone found sensitive personal information in the material.

Chapter 22

The End of the Rocky Flats Production Mission
or
Rocky Flats is Converted to a Day Camp for Nuclear Workers without a Mission

There have been numerous inaccurate reports about why Rocky Flats' production mission was terminated after the raid, and those inaccurate reports persist today. It follows the definition of "inculcation." Say a thing enough times, and soon everyone begins to accept it as true. It then becomes an urban myth. Many reports begin with, or contain words such as, "Rocky Flats was shut down because of illegal environmental activities." Those words are wrong on several levels. First, the raid and the Grand Jury investigation did not uncover illegal environmental activities. In fact the raid and the Grand Jury investigation didn't uncover anything that hadn't been previously reported by the site to the various regulators. Rockwell did plead guilty to violations of the water discharge permit and inadequate control of processes where sludge from the solar ponds was to be made into "pondcrete blocks." But neither of these were "illegal environmental activities." DOE did have a discharge permit, and Rockwell had been directed to clean out the solar ponds and make "pondcrete" from the sludge based on a compliance agreement between DOE and Colorado.

Rocky Flats shut down because pentagon planners decided it was no longer needed. President George H. W. Bush declared the end of the Cold War as relations eased with the Soviet Union. In January of 1992 he announced during his State of the Union Address the cancellation of plans to produce warheads for Trident Submarines, and the pits for those warheads was the only production mission remaining for Rocky Flats. In March of 1992 Energy Secretary Watkins announced the Rocky Flats mission would switch from building components for nuclear weapons to environmental restoration and waste management to prepare for eventual dismantling of the plant. (Colorado Council on Rocky Flats, January 1993, page 14)

Proving that I can master the art of understatement, I concede that the raid influenced decisions about Rocky Flats. Take the example of Building 460. The building was relatively new, and was full of high technology machinery to do precision machining of stainless steel parts. The Governor of Colorado announced that this was the perfect industrial operation for the environmentally conscious citizens of Colorado. Non-nuclear parts were machined by Q-cleared employees of Rocky Flats who

99

would continue to take their paychecks home and support Colorado communities. DOE looked at the support they had been given by the State of Colorado after the FBI raid, and, without ceremony, moved the stainless steel production process to Kansas City. However, the building wasn't wasted. It provided office space for large numbers of DOE employees and their subcontractors and waste storage capacity until the employees were laid off and the building was demolished several years later.

Much of Rocky Flats sat idle for years after the decision to end production of plutonium and other parts. The thousands of people working there began the process of waiting to see whether they would ever do what they had done before. There were, of course, those large numbers of DOE and their helpers doing oversight of this lack of activity. There also was a huge staff of environmental people monitoring every drop of water, creature, blade of vegetation, puff of air, or piece of dirt. Dangerous precedence was established by these activities. For example, environmental impact studies had to be completed and planned activities approved at several levels before a culvert could be scraped free of mud so it could drain properly. Part of the studies always involved assessment on potentially endangered creatures, such as the Prebles Jumping Mouse. People from Rocky Flats began to accept jobs in other agencies, and they became regulators. They obviously believed if protecting mice was good at Rocky Flats, it was good for Colorado, the nation, and the world. Development of various areas in the Front Range of Colorado was delayed for years while the habitat for a subspecies of mice was protected. An article titled, "Groups willing to tip scales back," said some biologists in the Fish and Wildlife Service were re-evaluating rulings, an environmental group was filing petitions, and a House of Representatives committee was holding hearings to figure out whether the mouse is an endangered species. (denverpost.com, August 2, 2007) I wonder whether the mice were confused or continue to be confused.

We should all be grateful the Colorado Water Quality Control Commission didn't apply the limits established for the non-drinking water drainages below Rocky Flats to sources of drinking water. We would probably have trouble finding enough water that would pass the purity requirements of water discharged from Rocky Flats. That would be especially true for Front Range reservoirs that receive their water from rivers flowing past old mine sites. The outcome of applying "Rocky Flats limits" throughout Colorado would perhaps have bankrupted municipalities with analytical costs and costs of additional water treatment, or maybe tap water would have become more expensive than bottled water. As an aside, I once mentioned the large costs of analyzing Rocky Flats water in casual conversation with a Colorado regulator. The response was interesting. "Nobody cares. It's just federal money."

Speaking of money, there was a move by the cities downstream of Rocky Flats to get some money for water projects. The cities had assured their citizens for decades the water coming from Rocky Flats was perfectly safe as drinking water supply. However, the raid on Rocky Flats and the fear it created presented opportunities that couldn't be ignored. One city demanded that DOE buy it a new water supply. Other cities demanded less. They only wanted basins built to capture and reanalyze Rocky Flats water that had been analyzed and approved for discharge. I began to see how the cities intended to take advantage of the circumstances created by the raid. The strategy was to extract money while DOE was in no position to negotiate.

There was a lengthy set of options developed on how water coming from Rocky Flats should be managed. I argued against the options being forcefully advocated by the cities, because I believed the price tag of over 100 million dollars wasn't justified. I even met privately with the senior person in DOE who was serving as site lead in deciding which options would be selected. I advised it might be wise to check whether it was a conflict of interest to also be on the city council of the city about to profit from the final decision while being the senior site DOE person involved in the decision. That city was about to have many tens of millions of dollars flow its way to buy a new water supply to replace a reservoir with a dam that needed repair and a water volume that wouldn't support the growth projections of the city. The city wanted a new water supply despite the ability to completely switch to Denver Water Department drinking water within 15 minutes. That contingency had been put in place with a $750,000 federal grant after the tritium incident (Denver Post, June 8, 1989a, page 11A). I argued the best option for managing the water was to restart the spray irrigation operations. That process had succeeded for years in significantly reducing the amount of water that had to be released from the site. My request was ignored.

Letters of the alphabet were assigned to options DOE was considering for managing water discharged from Rocky Flats, and the options the cities wanted selected were options "B" and "J". One of the people I worked with snickered that the more appropriate designation, considering how much money was about to be spent to solve a non-problem, was to simply leave out the "and," and call it the "BJ".

My attempts to prevent selection of the options preferred by the cities went unheeded, despite the solid evidence the quality of the water did not justify the multi-million dollar solution, and Congress approved the money. Congress also passed a special bill that gave the projects exemptions from the National Environmental Policy Act (NEPA), which was established in 1970, to assure government projects were properly evaluated for environmental impacts. Rocky Flats had to perform NEPA assessments for even the smallest of projects. One example I've previously given was the requirement to do one of the assessments before mud could be removed from a surface water pipe to allow runoff water to flow through the pipe. There are two possibilities as to why Congress exempted the water management and water supply options from NEPA. Perhaps they believed building new pipelines to move water across mountains and installing catch basins in the ditches below Rocky Flats would have less environmental impact than cleaning mud out of a drainage pipe. More logically, I had been given another lesson in the meaning of political advantage.

I was at a public meeting one night when one of the mayors began telling the audience the dam of a uranium tailings holding pond at the Colorado School of Mines campus was at risk of failing. The uranium-contaminated water would dump into Clear Creek if the dam failed. I was familiar with the problem, because Rocky Flats had been contacted and had promised to provide all available resources to help respond if needed. That's why I was surprised to hear the Mayor say, "This threat is exactly why we need Congress to approve the money for the proposed Rocky Flats water options."

My surprise was based on the knowledge Rocky Flats had nothing to do with the problem. The pond and water were part of the operations of the Colorado School of Mines Research Institute (CSMRI). I was also surprised because the "proposed Rocky Flats water options" would not help if the tailings dam failed. The water would have gone into Clear Creek, and the proposed catch basins would not have captured that water. I privately told the Mayor after the meeting I was disappointed to hear the statement. You will note I didn't say I was surprised, only that I was disappointed.

I wasn't the only one learning new lessons in politics. The EG&G managers brought in when Rockwell was thrown out were also learning. They had gotten off to a bad start when they first arrived. They traveled around the site telling people that DOE had said Rocky Flats workers either hadn't been adequately trained to do their work or they weren't properly motivated. A joke began to circulate soon after EG&G's arrival. The joke starts with a new EG&G manager telling a Rocky Flats employee, "I've been told that you don't know how to do your job, or you aren't motivated. What do you think?" The Rocky Flats employee responds, "I don't know, and I don't care." There were other stories about EG&G managers going to the workers and saying, "We're here to help you figure how to do your job properly and put together some proper procedures on the required steps. Tell us how you do your job so we can get started with the documentation." The workers are said to have responded, "No, you've already told me I don't know what I'm doing. You tell me what to do as you begin to write your procedures."

I was sitting in a meeting with a senior EG&G executive about six months into their contract. There were discussions about problems being faced and possible solutions. The conversation focused on DOE rejecting every suggested approach to solving a problem. The senior EG&G executive leading the meeting pushed back from the table with a look of consternation. "You know, I'm beginning to think Rockwell wasn't the problem here." I privately thought, "A stroke of genius can strike almost anyone, given enough time." I would be remiss if I didn't add that this person and EG&G both would prove that lessons can be learned and remembered by some in dealing with DOE. I was an observer in a meeting where senior DOE officials were telling the same EG&G manager to reduce the size of a requested budget based on anticipation that some regulatory environmental requirements would be renegotiated. I respected the manager's intelligence and tenacity for holding firm that any changes in the budget request would have to come after the renegotiation, and held that position despite intense and threatening behavior by DOE. I never heard of any changes in regulatory requirements, or that they were being renegotiated.

Fast-forward a few years: EG&G was replaced by a conglomerate company called Kaiser-Hill. EG&G walked away (maybe a Denver Post editor would say they "skedaddled" the same way Rockwell's' departure was described). They told DOE they no longer wanted to manage DOE facilities at Rocky Flats or anywhere else. They joined the lengthy list of multinational companies that recognized the wisdom Dow Chemical had displayed when they told ERDA, the son of AEC and father of DOE, they were not interested in a contract where ERDA made the decisions and the operating contractors would be the implementers. My guess is that Rockwell is the company that admires that wisdom more than any other.

Who manages Rocky Flats now means less with each passing day. Rocky Flats is an open area. All is gone except for the retirement and health benefits left behind for thousands of people, and perhaps a few lawsuits. Thank goodness there was a decision to keep the "buffer zone" of native high mountain prairie intact and undeveloped. That's a good thing Rocky Flats accomplished, because there are too few places like that remaining. Another positive impact of Rocky Flats is the thousands of families that were able to live near the place and be financially secure. This includes the people who worked there during production and all those who were able to work to retirement in the decade after the production mission was ended. I fit in both categories. Others who had good jobs because of Rocky Flats included the overseers, regulators, and consultants. Who knows how many people prospered in the neighborhoods around Rocky Flats because of the billions of dollars that flowed through the place over its 50-some years?

I realize there are those who would say it wasn't worth it, and that March 23, 1951 headline in the Denver Post, "There's Good News Today. U.S. to Build $45 Million A-Plant Near Denver" got it all wrong. Some will argue that the mission of the place was wrong, and the legacy of all those missiles containing the parts built at Rocky Flats is the proof. They probably would also add something about spewing of radiotoxic materials. I submit in response that independent studies found that the reports issued by Rocky Flats accurately presented environmental monitoring data. DOE gave Colorado five million dollars to do an independent study staffed by a dozen experts with impressive credentials following the FBI raid. Critics of Rocky Flats who alleged they knew of places where there had been illegal disposal were welcomed to join the study and share their knowledge. One of the reports published as a result of the studies included some fascinating statements.

"The records clearly indicate recognition of the need to control and limit radionuclide releases since the beginning of plant operations, driven by a combination of economic, national security, and health concerns. The extensive reviews failed to identify any historical evidence of undocumented or unmonitored routine airborne releases of radionuclides from the plant to the off-site environment, and this was generally true for waterborne releases with a few exceptions."

The report also contains the statements, "Review of historical accidents and incidents at the plant site led to the identification of voluminous amounts of information documenting small fires, spills, injuries, and incidents leading to property damage. However, none of the documentation indicated the occurrence of any previously unreported major events potentially impacting the off-site public." (Chemrisk, August 1992)

The Denver Post had an article titled, "Flat's neighbors reassured. Study: Radioactive leaks posed no unusual risks". The article said, in part, "A $5 million state study yesterday confirmed what the federal government has claimed for decades: Radioactive leaks from the Rocky Flats nuclear weapons plant have posed no unusual heath risks for metro Denver neighbors...Even vocal environmental critics of Rocky Flats said they were startled by the minimal health consequences of living downwind from the troubled U.S. Department of Energy complex...'I'm surprised by the results....The plant was lucky more radiation wasn't released and the people of Colorado were darn lucky too'...Researchers found that three significant Rocky Flats leaks....created a total radioactive dose of 10 millirems over four decades. That 40-year release is roughly equal to the amount of radioactivity in a single chest X-ray. The typical Denver resident gets 350 millirem per year of radioactivity just by living in Colorado..." (Denver Post, October 22, 1993, page 1A)

I disagree with one part of the article: The plant wasn't "lucky." The people who worked at the plant knew the hazards, respected the need to control the materials, and succeeded in protecting the surrounding areas though their professional, dedicated efforts. It wasn't an accident that the materials processed at Rocky Flats got away in such tiny quantities. It wasn't luck that caused environmental samples to be collected and analyzed from the start of operations, regardless that there were no laws requiring such sampling and analysis in the early decades of operations. It wasn't luck that resulted in ground water monitoring wells being installed at Rocky Flats as a good environmental monitoring practice decades before they became required by regulations. It wasn't luck that caused holding ponds to be installed at Rocky Flats and managed in cooperation with the local cities and the State. The reason Rocky Flats left such a remarkable legacy was because the people who worked there strived to do the right thing. On the subject of luck, Thomas Jefferson was quoted as saying "I find that the harder I work, the more luck I seem to have."

Another article titled, "Report says Rocky Flats is not a health hazard," confirms the positive Rocky Flats legacy. It summarizes a 130-page report from the Agency for Toxic Substances and Disease Registry, part of the Centers for Disease Control and Prevention. (dailycamera.com, September 15, 2004). It states that on-site contamination of the former industrial area won't be a problem "so long as site access is restricted, and that off-site surface contamination is "far lower than levels associated with adverse health. It concedes there is a theoretical risk of inhaling plutonium, but cancer risk "might, in fact, be zero."

I am curious about reports and studies such as these. I've written earlier that any new person or organization that studied anything about Rocky Flats and reported finding nothing new was judged by Rocky Flats critics to have joined the conspiracy. I wonder how the critics responded when the studies, including the one they supported done by the State, reached the conclusion there was nothing to find. There continue to be reports portraying the site as having left a dangerous legacy despite the evidence to the contrary. There are also occasional accusations that people who worked there committed environmental crimes. One recent article referred to "environmental and other crimes." The "other crimes" weren't defined, and I have no clue as to what the author was considering. I'm curious whether the author knew either. (DenverPost.com, March 26, 2006)

Chapter 23

Consensus

or

The Best Way to Spend the Most Money Over the Longest Possible Time

The loss of production mission at Rocky Flats created an unusual situation. The workers were well paid and had great benefits, but there was no job satisfaction that could be derived from the production of anything. Management of the site evolved into the least efficient possible process, and this was called "consensus building." Management based on consensus works only if you have unlimited amount of money and time, and you don't have any milestones to achieve. It is true the demolition of the site was eventually completed decades ahead of original estimates. I believe that was achieved because someone noticed a budget of over half a billion a year was being burned with no apparent mission other than maintaining the facilities and keeping a few thousand people off the streets. The prediction in the early 1990s by the ex-Admiral who was the Secretary of Energy that 4,000 people would soon lose their jobs at Rocky Flats didn't come true in that decade, although Kaiser-Hill did announce a layoff of about 1,500 people when they took over the site. Very few of those people left the site; they just lost their full-time salaried employee positions and were forced into third-tier subcontract jobs that came without benefits.

A Government Accounting Office (GAO) group visited the site in the mid-1990s to see how the money flowing into Rocky Flats was being spent. They toured what had been the production facilities, and saw no one in those areas. There were many people walking around outside, and the horseshoe pits were full of participants. (One environmental manager I worked with in the late 80s and early 90s once observed the only proven health effect of working with plutonium was it created an uncontrollable urge to pitch horseshoes.) The tour passed the 750 cafeteria, and it was full of people, and most of them were playing cards. (My guess is the dominant game was cribbage. Working at Rocky Flats must have made you want to play that card game when you weren't able to get to the horseshoe pits.) The story continues that GAO told DOE to get on with what should be done with the site, or the money was going to dry up. It was decided to give Kaiser-Hill a performance based contract to tear the place down much faster than anyone had predicted was possible. My perception is the people working at Rocky Flats were thrilled to once again have a mission, and were just as pleased that the decision was made to retrain the aging work force to be demolition workers instead of training and bringing in a younger, much more physically fit group that could have worked faster and probably safer. I say "probably safer" because there would be fewer muscle and joint pains among a younger group of workers. New people would have required training to work in areas contaminated with radioactivity, but the older workers they would have replaced hadn't known those skills when they first came to Rocky Flats either. That's all silly speculation anyway, because the several thousand Rocky Flats workers were a strong political force, and no one was going to suggest replacing them. The good news is that there were only a few years of inactivity before someone noticed there should be some kind of return for the half billion dollars being spent annually.

DOE relied on building consensus with all the various factions at Rocky Flats, and those factions often did not have the desire to quickly resolve problems as their primary motivator. I had a front row seat to watch bad decisions being reached by the consensus building process. One problem that was solved by consensus was what to do with tens of thousands of 55-gallon drums of trash, consisting of materials such as the contaminated coveralls and various kinds of plastics and paper. Some of this material had been stored in the drums since the days of decontamination following the 1969 fire, so I had put some of that material into some of those drums. A high technology incinerator, called a fluidized bed incinerator, had been installed in 76 building for the purpose of burning these materials. The process would reduce trash in the thousands of drums into a small amount of ash. Critics quickly began to attack the idea. The criticism focused on the risks to people downwind of Rocky Flats from dioxin, a chemical proven lethal to horses that is a by-product of high temperature chemical reactions. Risks, or perceived risks, from dioxin have been used to prevent incineration at any number of locations.

The dioxin argument didn't seem to be gaining much traction in trying to keep Rocky Flats from operating the incinerator, since there weren't many chemicals that would be involved that might result in dioxin being produced as a trace by-product. The design information for the system, to include the multiple effluent cleaning processes, was sent to the United States Center for Disease Control for an independent assessment of risk to anyone downwind. A public meeting was held to present the information. A technical person told the assembled audience there was one chance in a quadrillion (in other words, no risk at all) the effluent from the incineration would cause one person to have health problems. This detailed presentation was followed by a short statement from one of the professional Rocky Flats critics. My memory of what was said went something like this:

"These people think we're stupid. They're going to burn their unwanted plutonium in an open 55-gallon drum while stirring the fire to get rid of the radiotoxic ash. And they think we're stupid enough to believe that's safe."

The next day DOE announced they wouldn't use the incinerator, because "a consensus on its safety cannot be achieved." It isn't important what DOE knew or believed. What was important is that DOE had decided to "manage by consensus," which means (in my opinion) they were not going to take any risk of making any kind of management decision that would expose them to criticism. Why should they risk making a management decision and the need to defend it? Wouldn't it be better (from their perspective) to say they were trying to build consensus. The only risk was that the overall project would last much longer, require much more money, and require that the DOE oversight would have to last longer, which would extend their careers.

The dishonesty of the criticism voiced at the public meeting was remarkable. But even more remarkable was DOE's willingness to cave in to statements that had no truthful basis and their unwillingness to expose the dishonesty of the statement. The incinerator was designed to safely dispose contaminated cloth, paper, and plastic; it certainly wasn't designed to dispose plutonium. It was a carefully designed, fully contained system, and not a 55-gallon drum in the open. Gas emissions from the operation were to pass though four sets of high efficiency filters before they left the stack. The process wouldn't have been unsafe, and it would not have put anyone at risk.

The incinerator was never used for its designed purpose of efficiently reducing trash to ash. The more than 70,000 drums would be stored for years and would eventually be transported to New Mexico during a ten-year period for burial about a half mile deep in a salt bed. Critics tried unsuccessfully to stop that disposal process also, but it was the last remaining option, and DOE had to defend it. The cost to prepare the drums for transportation, load them in huge canisters, transport them on the highway to New Mexico, and bury them in the underground salt was of course funded by taxpayers. Carefully engineered and regulated incineration would produce a relatively small number of drums requiring shipment and disposal, but that was not to be. It was a glorious victory for consensus. I'll bet consensus continues to be used to solve contentious issues by many governmental agencies, and they probably brag about it. It is absolutely the best process to support the non-management method of bureaucracy that assures decision-makers won't be held accountable for any kind of decision, that the process will take the longest possible time, and the most money can be spent. In my opinion, that is the most disturbing legacy of Rocky Flats.

Chapter 24

Congratulations to the Critics
or
Appeal to Emotions When the Facts Aren't Effective

I've observed that technical people usually lose debates with critics. Technical people persist in presenting information and data in a language of math and science, and the eyes of people in the audience glaze over. It doesn't take much experience for a critic to learn it is more effective to say something easy to understand that creates a quick, emotional response. The technical person intently prepares by gathering all the data, assessing it, summarizing it, and readying it for presentation. This detailed preparation invariably identifies uncertainties, even though the uncertainty might be tiny to insignificant. A technical person challenged to declare whether something is completely safe will not do so, since there is nothing that is 100 percent safe. A good critic only has to say something simple that creates doubt. The critic wins the argument with minimal effort.

I recall one of the times this lesson was aptly demonstrated. I was watching a news report about the accident at Three Mile Island, which happened during the time I was gone from Rocky Flats. Various people were being interviewed, and a technical person from the operating organization was trying to reassure people releases from the nuclear reactor accident were small and that there was no cause for concern. The next person interviewed was introduced as a nuclear physicist, a person I recognized as an ardent critic of nuclear power. He said something close to, "These people are telling you there's no risk. That's a lie. The amount of radiation is equivalent to what would be measured after detonation of a nuclear weapon."

I was astonished and confused. What could this person be talking about? Then I remembered the environmental organization at Rocky Flats was directed to begin special air sampling and analysis after the Chinese set off an atmospheric nuclear test. We would detect a tiny but measurable increase in atmospheric radiation levels a few weeks after the blast.

What does this mean? A highly educated person with impressive professional credentials told a concerned audience the amount of radiation released was what would be measured after detonation of a nuclear weapon. People would have images of Hiroshima after the nuclear blast. It is unlikely they would think the person was referring to the amount of radiation carried into the United States by the upper winds from an atomic blast in China weeks earlier. However, I'm certain the desired uncertainty was created. There were undoubtedly people who concluded the officials from Three Mile Island trying to reassure them were lying. The data had been honestly presented by the technical person, and there wasn't a risk. What the critic said was technically accurate, completely disingenuous, and equivalent to shouting "fire" in a crowded theatre when there was no fire.

One of my favorite political cartoons was about Three Mile Island. A person was shouting, "What do you mean we exaggerate the risks of nuclear power? What about Twelve Mile Island?"

The day following the Three Mile Island accident and a long evening of television coverage, a gleeful coworker approached me. This was a person I had argued with frequently about the wisdom and value of nuclear power. We discussed the accident for a bit, until I observed the person seemed quite pleased about the accident.

"Yeah, it's just a shame it didn't kill some people."

"What?"

"If some people had died, it would have been even better proof we are right."

I thought for a moment, and then replied, "I want you to listen to me very clearly. I am going to tell you something, and this will be the last time I speak to you. You are despicable. You argue you're against nuclear power because it can harm people's health. But you wish people would die to give you the satisfaction of proving you're right. I've heard of people believing the end result justifies the means, but I've never heard a more disgusting example than this one." I'm hopeful most people who oppose nuclear power wouldn't condone a dishonest or unethical approach to supporting their opinions.

I recall an example of using disingenuous information designed to create doubt about information that was published by a DOE site. A report had been released about groundwater monitoring results at a site in Idaho. A critic announced it had been learned the site was keeping two sets of results, inferring or accusing the intent was to hide results the site didn't like. There were two sets of data, but the explanation was not as exciting as the accusation. A manager had heard regulations required the monitoring wells to be pumped to allow a fresh inflow of groundwater before samples were collected. The fresh inflow was to be sampled and analyzed and the results of that analysis reported. The manager was curious what was in the "stagnant" water in the well before the pumping, and requested that water to be sampled, analyzed, and reported internally. Results from the samples collected according to regulatory requirements were the ones used to file required reports. I saw some reports about the original accusations in the newspapers, but never saw anything about the explanation.

I've observed examples of critics using words intended to appeal to emotions to support anti-Rocky Flats beliefs. One of the Rocky Flats health physicists gave an hour-long presentation summarizing annual environmental monitoring results at a public meeting at Front Range Community College. The conclusion was that someone living at the plant boundary breathing the air at the plant boundary and drinking water out of the ditch where it left the site (health physicists tend to use worst case scenarios, even if they aren't credible) would have only a tiny increase in radiation exposure compared to exposure to natural background radiation from living in Colorado. I thought the presentation was impressive.

The meeting was opened to questions and comments. First up was one of our most dependable critics, who began with the usual comment, "Radiotoxic pollutants spewing from more than 27 vents..."

The evening news on television had a story about the meeting, and the only video shown was of the critic saying, "Radiotoxic pollutants spewing from more than 27 vents..." Fifty people at the meeting heard the presentation by the health physicist describing the minimal risks of Rocky Flats operations. Thousands of people watching television heard about "radiotoxic pollutants spewing..." The facts were evidently too long and boring to be newsworthy, while the words, "radiotoxic pollutants spewing..." undoubtedly made for a more interesting news report.

I continue to believe some Rocky Flats critics added value by constantly challenging us. I have a different opinion of those who simply used repetitive inflammatory words at whatever meeting they happened to be attending.

Chapter 25

Evidence of a Remarkable History

or

Amazing Accomplishments, Little Impact

Speeches at public meetings advocating people should fear Rocky Flats often included statements such as, "a tiny spec of plutonium will kill you…" The statements haven't stopped with the end of Rocky Flats and the conversion of the site into an open field. One example was on a television show discussing a proposed Colorado House bill that would require people to sign informed consent waivers before entering the Rocky Flats refuge. One person said, "If there's plutonium—if you get a particle in there, you're going to die. It's out there; one tiny particle of it will kill you." (Colorado Inside Out Live, January 12, 2005) The controversy over whether people should be able to visit the refuge also generated an article titled "An Idyllic Scene Polluted with Controversy." A person quoted in that article said, "What if you breathe in a particle of plutonium or are exposed to gamma radiation and get lung cancer." Another critic said, "I don't believe there is an acceptable level of plutonium; it remains dangerous in even minuscule quantities." An official with the Fish and Wildlife Service countered with, "There is absolutely no reason to warn people about the place. The refuge is safe…." (Los Angeles Times, February 7, 2005) Another article advocating passage of the bill that was designed to emphasize the dangers left behind at the site, titled "A right to know," said there is danger created by tiny amounts of plutonium. "The stuff has a half-life of 24,400 years, meaning that even the tiniest particles of plutonium will be dangerously toxic long after the Untied States of America has ceased to be a memory." (Boulder Weekly, January 27-February 3, 2005, page 1)

Is it true that a tiny particle of plutonium will kill people? Sadly, it's too late to avoid that outcome if that is true. There is plutonium contamination in every inch of dirt and ice from the North Pole to the South Pole. There is plutonium contamination in and on every living creature. The only way to escape "the tiniest spec of plutonium" would be to somehow be propelled off and away from the earth without the assist of any vehicle. Of course the human body would have to be left behind also. All humans on earth have many billions or trillions of atoms of plutonium in their bodies. The concentration of plutonium in man has been continuously increasing since atmospheric weapons testing began in the mid-1940s. Analysis of organ tissues from "non-occupationally exposed cases" of deceased humans found average plutonium concentrations of

114

0.5-0.7 pCi/kg of tissue. (Moss and Campbell, June 1972) There isn't a living creature or the remains of anything that lived on the surface of the planet since the middle of the 1940s that isn't contaminated inside and out with plutonium. The worldwide contamination began with the Trinity blast in 1945, and life spans have increased significantly since then. Of course there are many reasons for that increase in life span, and I doubt plutonium contamination of every living soul has made people live longer. However, the fact that people haven't died more quickly certainly is not consistent with statements about lethal effects from tiny amounts of plutonium.

Of course it isn't just the living things on earth that is contaminated. The steel walls used to construct one of the rooms containing equipment that measured internal contamination of workers at Rocky Flats (called "body counters") had to be taken from ships made before atmospheric testing began. The other room was constructed using steel from old trolley cars. Steel made after the testing began would have had sufficient radioactive contaminants to interfere with the counts. (Rocky Flats Endvision, September 3, 2004, page 7)

How much plutonium has been released to the atmosphere beginning with the culmination of the Manhattan project and the Trinity blast? The task force established to study Rocky Flats after the tritium incident in 1974 reported 300,000 to 500,000 curies of plutonium released worldwide by atmospheric weapons tests. That calculates to be between 9000 and 15,000 pounds of plutonium that had been released into the atmosphere by the time of that study. (Colorado Department of Health, October 1, 1975)

(I will provide a link depicting all of the nuclear detonations titled "1945-1998" by Isao Hashimoto. The link was active as of August 2010.)

www.ctbto.org/specials/1945-1998-by-isao-hashimoto/

Most of the plutonium released during atmospheric testing will already have been washed out of the air by rain or snow. The highest levels of plutonium from fallout in Colorado will be in the mountains where there is the largest accumulation of snow each winter. Snow is evidently quite efficient in washing plutonium from the atmosphere.

There are some who advocate that exposure to low levels of radioactive material is not harmful, since the evolution of man has taken place in the presence of radioactivity. I assure you those of us who worked with plutonium routinely strived to keep exposure as low as possible. I also will hazard a guess the people who worked at Rocky Flats understood and respected the risks from plutonium exposure better than most. The reports that we weren't careful with controlling plutonium releases are not based on facts. Anyone who worked there should have pride in the record of routine environmental achievement by the site. Studies by the State of Colorado completed over several years of effort after the raid estimated that there were 0.087 to 0.25 curies total airborne releases from Rocky Flats vents resulting from "routine operations" during the 40 years of production. (RAC Task 6, September 1999) There are about 14 grams of plutonium in a curie, so 1 to 3 grams of plutonium, or 0.04 to 0.11 ounces of plutonium were released out of the vents during "routine operations" over the entire history of Rocky Flats. It has been said there were tons of plutonium in Rocky Flats inventories and processed every year. An average of 0.006 ounces of plutonium being lost from the vents per year is a remarkably tiny number considering there were tons being processed.

I'm not forgetting that the data reported in the Colorado study about the 1957 fire in Building 71 and the 903-pad indicates there were several ounces (between 2 and 25) of plutonium released. (RAC Task 6, September 1999) I will assure you that critics will say that was too much. I will also assure you that I agree. No one who worked at the site wanted plutonium released. That attitude and the safety practices followed by the people who worked there are why such a small amount of the stuff was released from routine operations.

I have often heard people say all plutonium has been made by man. There were thousands of pounds of plutonium produced in the "natural reactor" of water pockets in uranium deposits in Africa about 1.8 billion years ago. Man used reactors to produce plutonium for Trinity and all the nuclear devices produced since then, but nature made significant amounts of plutonium long before man discovered how to replicate the process. Anyone interested in how plutonium was made by nature should search "Oklo Phenomenon."

Chapter 26

A Few More Facts

or

A Random Collection of Information and Opinions

I have some curiosity about the legacy of Rocky Flats now that it is gone. There are efforts to put together a Rocky Flats Museum, and private contributions are being solicited. (The web site is www.rockyflatscoldwarmuseum.org/.) There was an extensive Rocky Flats Reading Room at the Front Range Community College, but I understand the information is boxed and waiting for a decision on a final disposition. I'm interested in the outcome, because I believe the hundreds of unclassified documents, some of which are referenced in this book, is a solid indication environmental information was never hidden from the public.

I want to write about at least one subject that created news reports and negative reactions that baffled me and probably many other people at the site; someone gave a "tip" the plutonium building ductwork at Rocky Flats was contaminated. I imagine me and a few thousand other Rocky Flats workers thought nearly in unison, "of course the ducts are contaminated." The ductwork carried the contaminated air to filters that cleaned the air before it was released. The real scoop would have been if the ductwork hadn't been contaminated.

A related revelation was that the ductwork contained enough plutonium to build some number of atomic bombs. The reports inferred there was some security risk from the material in the ducts. It took years to recover the plutonium from the long mazes of ductwork as the buildings were being decontaminated and demolished. The media missed the real story about the ductwork. Maintenance of safety systems became bureaucratically complicated after Rocky Flats transitioned from knowledge and experience-based operations to procedure and documentation-based operations. Glove boxes were designed to be operated at negative pressure to prevent contamination release. The boxes contained "roughing filters" at the entry point to ductwork, and workers knew when these filters required replacement. There were gauges on the boxes that registered the vacuum being pulled on the box by the ventilation system. The workers could see by these gauges when the vacuum was diminishing. It also was easy to "feel" the strength of the vacuum when you pulled your hands out of the gloves, so you would know the roughing filters were filling up and needed replacement. In the "good old days" of knowledge and experience-based operations, the

117

workers could simply contact maintenance and the filter would be replaced.

It was nearly impossible to get anything done in the final years of Rocky Flats. Massive amounts of paperwork called "work packages" had to be completed and approved by multiple levels of management before any maintenance could be performed. The maintenance crews were powerless to act until they had a completed, reviewed, and signed package. The roughing filters were plugging even more, and the vacuum in the boxes was dropping while this bureaucratic, ritualistic dance was being performed and approved. One of the most frustrating parts of this process was the simple act of locating the people required to sign the package, because they were often scattered around the large site. Those who had to sign seldom actually read the packages beyond a quick scan, because they were required to approve many more of the documents than could be read in any detail. Procedures required a good vacuum before work could be performed. Perhaps more important was that people working in the boxes respected the need for a good vacuum, since it prevented them from becoming contaminated. When they judged the vacuum had dropped too much and the work package wasn't yet complete, they compensated. I've been told the workers would either pry one side of the roughing filter loose from where it was inserted or they would poke holes in the filter. Either approach resulted in an improved vacuum level inside the glove box and more contamination being pulled into the ductwork. The new bureaucrats didn't know the difference, because the workers weren't replacing filters until the mind-numbing stacks of paperwork were completed, reviewed, and signed by a dozen or more managers.

Probably the most infamous story in the years after bureaucracy was substituted for experience was about how many people it took to change a light bulb. The original joke was that it took five (insert the name of a group you like to tease, such as "salaried Rocky Flats employees") to change a light bulb. That's because one person held the bulb and the other four turned the person. It took many more people to change a light bulb at Rocky Flats beginning in the late 1980s and early 1990s. A light bulb in a criticality beacon was deemed to be part of a "vital safety system", and replacement required detailed work packages be developed, reviewed, and approved by numerous people. Someone leaked an internal memorandum about the process, and the resulting newspaper article said that it took "...at least 43 people 1087.1 hours to replace the light under a new management system...." (Denver Post, November 1, 1992, page 1 and 9A) Safety auditors were kept busy writing reports that the light in the beacon wasn't operational while the work package was being developed to replace it. The senior EG&G manager who wrote the leaked memorandum had intended to appeal to DOE to begin using a more common sense approach. After the newspaper article appeared the manager commented, "I'm beginning to think Rockwell wasn't the problem here." EG&G eventually gave up and pulled out of Rocky Flats and all other DOE work.

This occurred during the time Rocky Flats was redoing everything in preparation for the resumption of production operations, which of course never happened. It is difficult to write about the waste of resources caused by "resumption." The first building selected to undergo resumption was the 59 analytical laboratory. I can't recall how many months or years the resumption team worked to put all the procedures in place and train all the people in the new procedures. I do recall there was a proud announcement after the process was completed and the laboratory was allowed to begin analytical work. It was mentioned in the announcement that the cost of completing the resumption process was something in the vicinity of $23 million, and I know substantial additional costs incurred by the support organizations wasn't included in that estimate. What did it really cost? I don't know, but I do know the laboratory hadn't had any kind of actual safety problem that led to it being shut down. The people working there had known what to do and how to do it safely before resumption. The money was spent to solve a non-problem, and there are probably still some who are proud of what was done.

There were safety issues faced by Rocky Flats workers unique to facilities where nuclear materials are processed. I've had considerable time to think about the unavoidable fact that those of us who worked the "hot areas" were exposed to radiation. We worked there willingly, and we believed the work we were doing was important to our national defense. We have all heard several versions of the joke that commonly, or perhaps invariably, popped into the minds of people when they heard one of us say we worked at Rocky Flats or when our families told someone we worked there. The joke was (or maybe is) the one sentence question, "Do you glow?" or, to our families, "Do they glow?" Many of us worked in contaminated areas that the news media would naively call "infinity rooms," such as where I worked decontaminating after the 1969 fire. Many of us worked with highly radioactive materials, such as when I helped clean the old, and very "hot," plutonium ingots. And, no, I don't glow (although some of our Grandchildren might think that is disappointing).

Rocky Flats wasn't the only place where workers were building plutonium parts for nuclear weapons. There is a report titled "Experience with the first Soviet Nuclear installation (irradiation dose and personnel health)" from the Russian publication "Priroda" issued in February 1990 that gives some fascinating insights into the Soviet Union's weapons production. They tested their first atomic bomb at the Semipalatinsk test site in 1949. The Soviets believed, "This explosion took away the U.S. monopoly on nuclear arms, and the real threat of nuclear attack on our country, that had existed for nearly five years, was removed."

The report primarily presented details of radiation exposures for two Russian facilities, referred to as Facility A and Facility B. Facility A was a uranium-graphite reactor. Facility B was the radiochemical processing plant where plutonium and uranium were extracted from irradiated fuel. I believe both of these facilities were at a place called "Sorokovka" or "Forties Town" by the Russians and "the Kyshtym nuclear complex" by those who watched the Russian nuclear program for the United States. The town and complex weren't on any maps. You will probably see the connection I feel with the workers at these places when you read what the report said about the people working there. "Not only managers but also ordinary employees recognized dangers of working under elevated radiation impact. Nevertheless they realized the country needed nuclear arms desperately and often put their own safety at risk." (Nikipelov, February 1990)

The discussion of radiation exposure levels at the two Russian sites is startling. The people had very high exposures from 1948-1952, and then it was recognized the exposures had to be reduced. The measures to reduce exposures were implemented in 1953-1959. "As a result the irradiation situation was normalized and in 1960-1973 the radiation doses fell to within the international standards." The average annual radiation dose listed for Installation A ranged from 18.1 to 93.6 rem from 1948 to 1952. The averages for Installation B for the same time period ranged from 48.0 to 113.3 rem. Installation B undoubtedly had the most severe record of radiation-induced sickness. A total of 42.8 percent of the workers had exposures ranging from 100-400 rem in 1950-1951, the worst time period. There were 1.8 percent of the people who had more than 400 rem exposure that same year. The Nuclear Regulatory Commission (NRC) website glossary says an acute (short time period) dose 400 to 450 rem is expected to be a Lethal Dose (LD) for half the people within 30 days (LD 50/30). (nrc.gov, February 2007) The Soviets reported "The first cases of radiation diseases have been detected as early as the beginning of 1949" and "called for urgent measures to improve the working conditions. However it was extremely difficult to follow the norms limiting the irradiation of workers to replace the over irradiated ones and to train new specialists for this top secret complex and crucially important plant…"

The Russians established a limit of 15 rem per year in 1952. The limit at Rocky Flats when I first began to work there in 1969 was 5 rem per year, and that was reduced over time. For comparison with the Russians, my exposure at Rocky Flats totaled about 22 rem. I speculate that's probably higher than for many, or maybe even most, salaried people, especially managers. It is probably low compared to the hourly workers in the "hotter" areas of Rocky Flats, to include the recovery processing areas of 71. Individual exposure records are personal and confidential, as they should be, so that's as far as I can go in comparing exposures of people at Rocky Flats to those poor devils in Russia.

I suppose I'm obliged to answer a couple of likely questions. Yes, I've had two bouts of cancer, and no, I don't know whether working at Rocky Flats caused it.

*

Chapter 27

Cancer

I stared at the single word for quite a bit after I first typed it. It's an ugly word, and an ugly subject for me. I never wanted to write about it, but I've convinced myself I must to have an accurate story.

I've heard statements that were something like "You have cancer" twice, and the impact was immediate and extensive both times. The first time I heard it was after a suspicious mole was found to be a melanoma that had penetrated deep enough that odds of survival were less than 50-50. The second cancer was a cancerous lymph node found by my oncologist. Removal of all the lymph nodes in the groin and a few inches up found one more cancerous node.

Treatments after the first diagnosis were by self-injections of a chemical that was to improve the immune system. I was often very sick and weak, but was told there were indications the treatments worked. They didn't. Treatments after the second diagnosis, which gave me a survival chance of about 28 percent, lasted three years.

My family encouraged me to do the self-injection treatments after my second diagnosis, and I slowly became more accustomed to the effects. I can best describe the three years of treatments as similar to having low-grade flu combined with various levels of depression. I hated giving myself shots, even though the needles were tiny. I developed a little ritual that involved lying down after the injection, closing my eyes, and trying to relax. I would notice my respiration and pulse rates were elevated. I would concentrate on the pulse, and develop a mental image of the poisonous chemical I had injected flowing through the blood stream until a cell with a black center appeared. My mental picture was of the poison penetrating and killing the cancerous cell.

I completed the treatments, and I felt some guilt when the doctor told me, "It looks like you are going to make it." My thought, which I understand doesn't sound rational, was, "I don't know that I deserve taking one of the few slots of those who lives." I have been cancer-free for well over the 10 years required to mean I have the same risk as the average person.

I avoid the subject of health associated with Rocky Flats employment for two reasons. The first is that I am completely uncomfortable with discussing the experiences I just described. The second is that I don't want to insult fellow workers who are dealing with devastating diseases.

I want to reiterate I was well informed about health risks during my work at Rocky Flats. My opinion is that the worst health problems were caused by beryllium. Some people are very sensitive to beryllium, and develop berylliosis, a devastating lung disease, after exposure to minute amounts. What made beryllium even more frightening than plutonium was that it could not be immediately detected in the breathing air. Radioactive materials would set off alarms nearly instantly. You wouldn't know about beryllium exposure until much later and far too late. Those who preached that exposure to a tiny particle of plutonium would be toxic were talking about the wrong material.

What about plutonium? There is a continuing study of the twenty-six Manhattan Project workers who were involved in the original plutonium research, making parts, and assembling the first weapons at Los Alamos who were exposed to large amounts of plutonium. At least some of them were exposed in the "ice house," a building that had been previously used by the Boy Scouts to store ice collected in the winter. Plutonium parts were assembled in the open, on top of the tables, and not in glove boxes. Seven of the twenty-six individuals had died during the fifty years that followed compared to 16 deaths that would have been expected for people in the general population. The rate was also not elevated when this group was compared to large numbers of people working at Los Alamos who did not work in processing areas. Eight of the twenty-six workers had developed cancer, and three died of cancer. The underlying cause of death for the three was prostate, lung, and bone cancer. However, neither the numbers of cancers nor mortality rates were elevated compared to rates for the general population. (Volez, et al. October 1997) I attended at least one seminar about these studies as they were being developed. The speaker expressed that many were surprised lung cancer wasn't more prevalent among the Los Alamos workers, since they were provided an endless supply of free cigarettes.

What about the data for Rocky Flats workers? One study, which was completed over twenty years ago, found overall incidence of cancer was less for people who worked there than the general population. The study included 5,413 white male workers (most workers were white males, especially in the early years) who had been employed at least two years at Rocky Flats. The person who provided me a copy of the article wrote a note that said in part, "There has been a lot of review and analysis (cussing and discussing) of this paper and conclusions from the data." The abstract of the paper says, "Mortality...was investigated to measure risks from exposures to low levels of plutonium and external radiation. When compared with U.S. death rates, fewer deaths than expected were found for all causes of death, all cancers, and lung cancer. No bone cancer was observed. An excess of brain tumors was found...."

(Wilkinson et al., February 1987) The excess of brain tumors reported was one issue that was cussed and discussed, because all tumors, malignant and non-malignant, were used for comparison to the general population rate for malignant tumors. The person who sent me the paper warned against leaping to the conclusion that working with plutonium improves health (my simplistic words). The "healthy worker theory" is that Rocky Flats workers had lower incidences of cancer because production areas had very clean air; smoking wasn't allowed. Spending working hours in highly filtered, smoke-free air in conjunction with an excellent health insurance program resulted in healthier people. I can also assure you I wasn't under-fed while I worked at the Flats, and from my observations walking through the locker room during shift changes I can safely say the same was true for most of the other men. We had excellent health benefits, which gave us more opportunities to see doctors who advised we should stop smoking and cut back on calories.

Most reports about health risks from working with plutonium such as the ones referenced above were in specialty scientific journals that have a relatively small distribution. However, I found at least one article titled, "Plutonium cancer risk 'negligible'" in a general distribution newspaper published shortly after the raid at Rocky Flats. "Even if allegations prove true that the Rocky Flats plant illegally spewed radioactive plutonium, the risk of cancer to workers and nearby residents probably is negligible, several top radiation and health experts said yesterday." (Denver Post, June 28, page1A, 1989)

I'm not saying working with plutonium was without risk; it certainly wasn't a good idea to breathe the stuff or have it injected into a wound. I also understand that statements like "...generally...lower overall risk of cancer," don't mean much to a person who is dealing with the disease.

The stories dominating the news about Rocky Flats the last few years are about the battle between workers who are sick and the government agencies assigned to compensate people who more likely than not became sick because of their work. I understand this is a very difficult issue, and I'm not going to judge what is right or wrong. And that's all I have to say about that, although I'll provide a link that seeks support for Rocky Flats employees (http://www.rockyflatsnuclear.com).

Chapter 28

Who Committed Crimes?
or
Who Should Pay?

There was a lawsuit filed by property owners downwind of Rocky Flats in 1989 after the raid, and a majority of the jury issued a verdict in 2006 finding that the plaintiffs should be awarded $553.9 million dollars because of damages from plutonium contamination. (Denver Post, February 15, 2006, page 1A) The jury decision was not unanimous. Some of the jury members apparently were influenced to support the plaintiffs by a rehash of the allegations in the search warrant that had authorized the raid. The opinions of some others apparently were swayed to find for the defendants based on results of studies by a variety of agencies that found no significant impact from the plant. One juror in the latter camp pleaded with the judge to intercede and stop bullying by some of those who wanted to reach a verdict for the plaintiff, but the judge refused to listen. The bullying persisted until the person was driven from the jury room on the fourth day and was removed from the jury by the judge. The absence of that person gave the jurors wanting to find for the plaintiffs the majority. Two pro-defense jurors later provided letters to the defense complaining about the deliberations. (Rocky Mountain News, September 2, 2006, pages 4A and 12A)

The amount of the award had grown with compounded interest to $926 million by the time the U.S. Circuit Court of Appeals in Denver tossed the verdict. The Appeals Court ruled that the jury had been given faulty instructions, and that the plaintiffs had not proven their properties had been damaged. (Denver Post, September 4, 2010, pages 1 and 24A.)

My opinion is that the failure of the government officials investigating Rocky Flats to admit they couldn't find evidence supporting the allegations in the search warrant is what caused the most damage. I submit the jury verdict in 2006 as proof of the toxic effect the government's actions on the reputation of the site and the people who worked there. Even the Denver Post article that reported that 2006 verdict had been overturned predictably included the statement that Rocky Flats was "…closed in 1989 for safety and environmental reasons…." The irony is that the article also stated that Rocky Flats had caused no damages to health or properties.

Many people who worked at Rocky Flats were uncomfortable expressing their opinions about the raid and ensuing investigation. Perhaps that has changed with the passage of time. A person who had worked in the environmental organization and was respected by people both on and off the site responded to a message I sent inquiring about the raid.

"I do remember my feelings at the time. I too was fearful, and I also was very angry....I had one interview with an FBI agent...and I told him...I felt very comfortable with what I knew and with what I had done, but was very uncomfortable with a legal system that could initiate this kind of criminal raid at Rocky Flats. I told him I did not believe that anyone at the plant could have done anything to justify this type of investigation."

"The questions focused on non-rad issues, dealing with illegal waste discharges (midnight dumping) and illegal operation of the incinerator. If my memory is correct, I told him that it appeared to me that there would have been no reason to do either: the government was paying the tab for waste treatment and disposal. There was no profit to be gained in not doing it correctly and there was ample sampling data to back that up."

"I remained in a rage about the raid for years later. I was finally able to let go after a conversation during a carpool to CDPHE...I don't remember everyone who was in the car, but it included DOE and contractor environmental folks. One of the relatively new people with DOE...had previously worked for the EPA during the time of the raid...wasn't involved in the raid, but heard about it tangentially in conversations... *(It) was stated very clearly that the EPA knew within a few days that the really serious allegations in the search warrant (midnight dumping and illegal operation of the incinerator) were fallacious. But...they couldn't admit to the error because of all the publicity and high visibility of the raid. That's why they continued the investigation."* (Emphasis added)

"For some reason, hearing someone who'd been with EPA admit what I had always believed allowed me to let my rage go. I still get worked up in talking about it, but it was no longer the extreme emotional burden that it had been."

The fact that a former EPA employee had told a Rockwell employee that it was known within a very short time that the allegations in the Search Warrant were incorrect, and that the raid continued rather than to admit it was unjustified was reported by Rockwell to the Justice Department. (United States District Court (Limine) November 10, 1997, page 37)

Rocky Flats employees and investigators weren't the only people who believed the raid was a mistake. I located a reference in an article describing a DOE conference held in 1995 that said the Governor of

126

Colorado had strongly criticized the raid, "...saying it resulted in false allegations of wrongdoing that needlessly damaged government credibility about operations at the plutonium facility." "He also disclosed, for the first time, that within 24 hours of the raid he had concluded the midnight burning charges were not true. He said that due to the complexity and number of people required to operate the incinerator, 'I concluded they just couldn't have pulled it off without it being known'." He said he kept quiet about his doubts because no one would have believed him at the time. "You don't go against infrared photos, the FBI, and the Environmental Protection Agency." (The Energy Daily, Wednesday, August 16, 1995)

I located the referenced document searching archives in the Rocky Flats Museum facility. The collection of media reports that included the document did not have any Denver newspaper articles about the Governor's statements, and searches of Denver paper archives have found nothing yet. The press can shape public opinion by what they chose to not publish as well as by what they do publish. This would be a classic example, if the major Denver newspapers chose to not print a story on these startling statements by the Governor.

A copyrighted article written by Barry Siegel in the Los Angeles Times Magazine, titled "Showdown at Rocky Flats." (Los Angeles Times Magazine, August 15, 2003, pages 1-9) presents an excellent summary of several complex components of the overall story. It provides an analysis of the raid, the reactions of the Grand Jury members after the plea bargain, and a Congressional hearing that resulted from their outrage. (I purchased a copy by calling 1-800-788-8804, which was the number for the Los Angeles Times Archives and Research Service.) Mr. Siegel judged, "The grand jurors' passion arose...from an abhorrence of hypocrisy and double standards..." The information and quotes included in the next several paragraphs are taken from his article.

The Grand Jurors wrote their own report as they had been instructed to do when they were first given instructions by the judge. The Justice Department criticized their report, and Mr. Siegel agreed with the Justice Department. He wrote, "The prosecutors were right—the Grand Jurors undeniably had fashioned a simplistic report much more by moral outrage than legal rigor." However, the outrage expressed by the Grand Jurors brought on a Congressional hearing, and the Assistant U.S. Attorney testified under oath to that committee. He said, "They had expected to find rogue individuals saying, '(Let's) go bury it on the south 40,' but instead they'd found an 'institutional culture unchallenged by Congress or regulatory agencies.' The culture wasn't the result of one person in the

Energy Department, anymore at Rocky Flats or Rockwell. Was it fair 'to prosecute someone acting consistent' with his culture? 'How do you indict a culture'?"

"One grand juror now says... 'This was not a particularly strong criminal case. But this was a strong portrait of a public policy tragedy'."

"In truth, however, neither the contractor nor the regulatory agencies have any other choice. Legal means still do not exist to treat, dispose, or store the type of mixed hazardous wastes generated at Rocky Flat and other weapons plants. They never have. From the moment environmental laws such as RCRA were passed—or at least from the moment it was decided they applied to DOE facilities—plants such as Rocky Flats had to break the law if they were to continue operating. Rockwell knew this, DOE knew this, and the regulatory agencies knew this. So did Congress." (Note that this was remedied by the Compliance Agreement that stipulated how the wastes were to be managed.)

"In the end the Justice Department covered up not midnight incinerator burns, but a scathing critique of DOE and of all public policy."

I think an outburst from the Assistant U.S. Attorney in front of the Congressional committee when the investigation was being criticized would be a good place to end this. "Look, we wouldn't be here in this room if I hadn't decided to do Rocky Flats. There would be no Wolpe subcommittee investigation, no celebrated runaway grand jury. There are 16 DOE plants—Hanford and Savannah River are even worse than Rocky Flats. I don't see any EPA agents or assistant U.S. attorneys taking them on. Now we do, and we're criticized for it. The message is, it ain't worth it."

I agree. The investigation and raid didn't result in additional protection to the environment or people. It only resulted in an intense investigation of policy, and at huge costs in resources and money and with emotional costs to loyal citizens who had done what their country had asked them to do. No one liked the outcome. It wasn't worth it. It was known within a few days after the raid began there was no justification for the fear that it caused. The investigators chose to protect their reputations instead of admitting they had been mislead. I hope I would have been able to follow my own advice on what to do in difficult times if I had been in the shoes of the investigators. I hope I would have stopped the raid when it was learned nothing existed or was being done to threaten the environment or the neighbors of the site. I hope I would have then been able to face the consequences of the political embarrassment. I hope I would have taken the investigative team to Denver and called a press conference. I hope I would have had the courage to do the right thing.

Epilogue

or

Last Comments and Requests

I have considered possible readers and wonder about the reactions. The first possible readers I will mention are those who call themselves "investigative reporters." I hope some (one?) of you will be sufficiently curious about what I've written and the references to look into the story. I expect some of you will simply pull out the old stories, accept the misinformation that the Rocky Flats urban myths are true, and dismiss the ideas presented here. I hope one or some of you who will use the insight shown by the political cartoon from the Boulder Daily Camera published December 5, 1988. It has two frames, and the left frame is a drawing of four incoming missiles labeled "Warheads." The right frame is a drawing of a weapons plant with leaking nuclear waste labeled "Wartails." That cartoon thoughtfully presented the two arguments against Rocky Flats. Other political cartoons were simple cheap shots such as the one that appeared in the Westminster Sentinel dated simply 1990. It depicts a slovenly, scrubby-bearded, barefoot man wearing a shirt labeled Rocky Flats with a crushed beer can beside his chair. There are smoking radioactive waste containers in the front yard in the grass that needs to be mowed. A neighbor in the background is saying "No matter how much everyone works at cleaning up, there's always someone who ruins it for the whole neighborhood."

Another group of possible readers I will address includes the critics of Rocky Flats. I request that you consider the references I've provided before you reject everything I've written. And I request polite disagreement.

To the members of the Grand Jury, thank you for your service. You continued to meet your responsibility through a long and difficult process. You stood up for what you thought was right despite intense pressure, and I respect you for that. I think it was wrong if one or more of you gave information sealed by the court to the press, because, in my opinion, what had transpired did not justify breaking the law. I would be surprised if you aren't upset by some of what I've written. I'm hopeful some of you will read this and reflect on what you believe. I also hope we could have a civilized conversation, if we ever had that opportunity.

To the DOE, I worked with DOE people I respected and liked and others I preferred to avoid. There are those in the latter group who probably would say the feeling was mutual. I do not criticize everything DOE did during my time working for them, but there were actions by that bureaucracy that I will never forgive. I have written that DOE used self-criticism as a method of gaining budget approvals from Congress, and there is evidence to support that opinion. A Colorado Congressman called for an investigation of DOE for purposely overstating the extent of Rocky Flats safety problems to secure Congressional funding. This occurred after the Rocky Flats DOE Safety Director said DOE had "heightened" its description of safety problems in order to win $100 million for plant improvement. *"Unless you make it sound horrible, they're not going to fund it. You have to paint an exaggerated picture of why you need it. To get funded, that's the game, especially with budget issues."* (Emphasis added) (Rocky Mountain News, May 10, 1991) I can tell you people at Rocky Flats did not consider what was done to be a game. It is true that untold millions and possibly billions of dollars were obtained by releasing reports that significantly exaggerated environmental and safety problems. However, the harm caused by that approach cannot be measured. Contemplate the number of worthy projects that could have been funded with that wasted money. Also contemplate the damaged reputations of people who had once proudly dedicated themselves to completing the government–directed Rocky Flats mission. DOE was responsible for how Rocky Flats was operated and, in my opinion, was responsible for what led to the raid. The government, including DOE, took the shameful and cowardly approach of using Rockwell's willingness to protect the reputation of their employees to force a guilty plea. Parents and grandparents strive to teach children to make good decisions, and to take responsibility for their own actions if the results aren't good. I can only hope that current and future DOE leaders are and will be the kind of leaders who demonstrate the responsibility we strive to teach our children. I will express the same hope for the Justice Department.

To Rockwell, I often appreciated the leadership and support your managers gave. I respected several of them, and even liked some of them. There were others I avoided as often as practical. I know you learned the lesson a long list of multinational companies learned, including EG&G, the company that replaced you at Rocky Flats, that there is no reason to accept contracts managing DOE facilities. Don't take on the project, no matter how lucrative, if government officials are going to make the decisions and control the money. The government may have fooled you, but you demonstrated you are a company that deserves respect. You swallowed a very unfair pill to provide an out for others who didn't have the same kind of courage. I don't think I was one of the people being threatened with indictment, but I can imagine how that must have felt. You accepted the unprecedented burden of paying 18.5 million dollars in

130

fines that DOE was required to pay under contract. You agreed because you cared for your employees. You did the right thing for your people despite the damage it caused you, and I give you my sincere thanks.

The reactions I care most about are from Rocky Flats coworkers and my family. First, to my family, I apologize for all those years when you knew very little about where I worked and what I did there. Secrecy prevented me from talking about what I did in the early days. Then the place became so unpopular that it was uncomfortable for you to endure the criticism of others. You had to bear the burden of negative opinions about where I worked, and that was grossly unfair to you.

The high school child of a person I worked with wrote a paper about "good works of Rocky Flats" after doing some research by reading and interviewing various people. The paper discussed the positive economic impact of the site on the surrounding communities, the network of workers who volunteered in a broad variety of community activities, and the amount of money donated by people at the site to local charities. The teacher announced to the class the student was given a "B" for a very well written paper, "despite the fact it was full of lies."

My wife had an unhappy experience at a work seminar for nurses. A person representing a local hospice had given a presentation. One question was about how the hospice was funded. The presenter responded, "We get funding from many sources. You won't believe this, but our largest contributor is Rocky Flats." My wife asked the presenter why that would be difficult to believe. She told me I should call the people who decided which agencies and organizations should receive donations and tell them their generosity wasn't appreciated at that particular hospice.

Perhaps the worst example of the burden my family had to bear because of my work happened to our son. He was in the eighth grade, and had a social studies assignment that included describing his parent's careers. When the teacher heard I worked at Rocky Flats, the class was told something to the effect, "This student's father is the reason we are in danger from where he works and have to live in fear of nuclear attack caused by the place." I judge my son knew me well to not tell me about the humiliation he experienced from that teacher until years later. He probably also warned his sister to make up a fictitious place of employment if she were ever asked to same question. One researcher I worked with told his family to say he was a professor at Colorado University.

To Rocky Flats workers, some of us knew each other well, and many of us never encountered each other in the years we worked in that large, complicated place. I know you had different experiences than mine, and you could add many interesting stories about the plant. Some of the Union folks will not agree with my perceptions and opinions. I acknowledge that the strength of the Union benefited everyone. Salaried people gained the same benefits as the result of successful Union negotiations. I appreciated that. I believe many of the salaried people wished they had belonged to the Union when EG&G left and DOE insisted the new contract required about 1500 salaried employees had to lose their full-time employee benefits as they were being forced into being subcontractors. Those people had to feel even worse when DOE announced they had reduced the work force, knowing that the only reduction had been in the number of people who had full benefits.

People working at Rocky Flats in the 1970s and 1980s experienced the transition of being proud of where we worked to feeling uneasy as the reputation of the place decayed. We were uncomfortable to read and hear the numerous negative reports and to be questioned by our neighbors. The 1989 raid caused some or maybe many of you to believe criminal activities were going on somewhere at the plant away from your particular work area. I say to all of you, many, many millions of dollars spent by the investigators found no criminal activities. You should rethink any misgivings about our work at Rocky Flats. Our role in the Cold War was crucial, and you should be proud. I don't doubt for a moment there are those in the world who covet both our freedom and our wealth, and would attack us if it weren't for our strength and willingness to respond when threatened. It is evident those who judge us as weak by what they see on the evening news reports continue to pause when they reflect on our reactions to attacks. The motto, "Don't tread on me," continues to be an effective statement about our national attitude. We remain a powerful and free country, and our children and grandchildren will have freedom and opportunities as long as we have brave soldiers who are armed with the best weapons in the world.

References

Atomic Energy Commission, August 1969. "Report on Investigation of Fire – Building 776-777, Golden Colorado, May 11, 1969." Volume I.

Atomic Energy Commission, December 1, 1969. "Serious Accidents—Fire—Rocky Flats Plant—May 11, 1969." Issue No. 306.

Boulder Daily Camera, February 4, 1966, "Rocky Flats Plant Keeps Radioactivity Confined," no author listed, page 9.

Boulder Daily Camera, March 5, 1988, "DOE to extend Rockwell's contract to run Flats," Associated Press, Page 1A

Boulder Daily Camera, August 25, 1991, "Expert: Too much oversight," Gregory Todd, page 1D.

Boulder Daily Camera, November 1, 1992, "Light-bulb change a 43-person task," Associated Press, page 5B

Boulder Daily Camera, October 14, 2004. "Test on Flats deer show little radiation." Todd Neff, pages 1A-2A.

Boulder Weekly, January 6 – January 13, 2005. "Servant of the people." Jool Warner, pages 1-7.

Boulder Weekly, January 27 – February 3, 2005. "A right to know." Pamela White, pages 1-2.

Capel, Paul D., and Steven J. Larson, 2001. "Effect of Scale on the Behavior of Atrazine in Surface Waters." Environmental Science and Technology. American Chemical Society Publications, 35 (4), pages 648-657.

CDPHE, March 26, 2004. Letter to the Honorable Mark Udall. Douglas H. Benevento, CDPHE Executive Director.

ChemRisk, August 1992. "Reconstruction of Historical Rocky Flats Operations & Identification of Release Points." Project Tasks 3 & 4, Final Draft Report, prepared for the Colorado Department of Health.

Colorado Council on Rocky Flats, January 1993. "The Handbook on Rocky Flats."

Colorado Department of Health, October 1, 1975. "Lamm-Wirth Task Force on Rocky Flats." Robert D. Siek, et al.

Colorado Federal District Court, February 19, 1992. "Report of the Special Grand Jury 89-2 (Redacted)."

Colorado Inside Out Live, January 12, 2005. Peter Boyles, host, Television Broadcast Transcript, KBDI-TV (PBS) Channel 12 – Denver.

Dailycamera.com, September 15, 2004. "Report says Rocky Flats is not a health hazard." Todd Neff.

David, Bruce and Mark Cromer, November 2004. "Rocky Mountain Meltdown." Hustler Magazine, pages 1-5.

Denver Post, June 7, 1989. "Federal Agents raid Rocky Flats." Thomas Graf, page 1A.

Denver Post, June 8, 1989. "Rocky Flatheads." Woody Paige, page 7B.

Denver Post, June 8, 1989a. "Tests find no toxic water in suburbs below weapons plant." Mark Obmascik, page 11A.

Denver Post, June 13, 1989. "Investigation at Rocky Flats—Genetic-test chemical suspected in dumping." Michael Booth, page 2B.

Denver Post, June 15, 1989. "Old rumor of nuclear reaction in spotlight." Thomas Graf, pages 1A and 15A.

Denver Post, June 22, 1989. "200 protestors demand closing of weapons plant." J. Sebastain Sinisi, page 3B.

Denver Post, June 26, 1989. "Link between Flats' burns, winds probed." Thomas Graf, pages 1A and 8A.

Denver Post, June 28, 1989. "Plutonium cancer risk 'negligible' " Albuquerque, page 17A.

Denver Post, October 12, 1989. "U.S. raised ante to get EG&G to assume operation of Flats." Thomas Graf, page 9A.

Denver Post, January 4, 1990. "An Open Letter To Rockwell International From The People Of Colorado." F. Gilman Spencer.

Denver Post, October 24, 1990. "Morale at Flats dives, report finds." Associated Press, page 3B.

Denver Post, April 11, 1991. "Secret Settlement in Flats suit, Plant employees reported threat." Mark Obmascik, Pages 1 and 20A.

Denver Post, May 10, 1991, "Skaggs: False data at Flats a 'threat', " Robert Kowalski, page 3B

Denver Post, November 1, 1992, "Light-bulb change a 43 person task," Mark Obmascik, pages 1 and 9A

Denver Post, October 22, 1993. "Flats' neighbors reassured." Mark Obmascik, pages 1B and 5B.

Denver Post, December 19, 2004. "Water protection adrift." Miles Mofffeit and Theo Stein, pages 1A, 16A, and 17A.

Denver Post, February 4, 2005. "Crews begin cleaning up radioactive Flats ponds." Kim McGuire, page 1A.

Denver Post, January 29, 2006. "Drilling pursued at nuke test site." David Olinger, pages 1A and 23A.

Denver Post, February 15, 2006. "Flats plaintiffs due $554 million," Alicia Caldwell, page 1A and 6A.

Denver Post, February 12, 2007. "Release of nuke-site drilling study delayed." Nancy Lofholm.)

Denver Post, September 4, 2010, "Damages Tossed in Rocky Flats suit," Denver Post staff and wire reports, pages 1A and 24A

DenverPost.com, March 26, 2006. "Nukes of the future." Len Ackland.

DenverPost.com, August 2, 2007. "Groups aiming to tip scales back." Steve Lipsher.

Department of Energy (DOE), April 1980. "Environmental Impact Statement." Final Statement to ERDA 1545-D. Rocky Flats Plant Site, Golden, Jefferson Country, Colorado.

DOE, 1996. "Project Plowshare." Office of Environmental Management, BEMR.

Edward A. Putzier, "The Past 30 Years at Rocky Flats Plant," November 1982

George Voelz, et al., October 1997. "Fifty Years of Plutonium Exposure to the Manhattan Project Plutonium Workers: An Update." Health Physics 73(4): 611-619.

Johnston, Wm. Robert, March 4, 2006. "SL-1 reactor excursion, 1961." Database of radiological incidents and related events—Johnston's Archive, pages 1-2.

Kaiser Hill Company and DOE, 2003. "Rocky Flats History."

KBTR radio transcript, "Charges of radioactive pollution against Dow Chemical Company are in the news this afternoon," Reporter Gene Towne, July 17, 1970

LewRockwell.com, November 11, 2006. "Courts of the State – and the State of Justice." William L. Anderson.

Los Angeles Times Magazine, August 8, 1993. "Showdown at Rocky Flats." Barry Siegel, pages 12-18 and 48-51.

Los Angeles Times Magazine, August 15, 1993. "Showdown at Rocky Flats." Barry Siegel, pages 1-9.

Los Angeles Times, February 7, 2005. "An Idyllic Scene Polluted with Controversy." David Kelly, pages 1-2.

McKinley, Wes, and Caron Balkany, Esq., 2004. The Ambushed Grand Jury. Apex Press: New York.

Moss, W. D., and E. E. Campbell, June 1972. "Plutonium Concentration in Tissues in a General Population." Health Physics, 22(6): 933.

Nikipelov, Boris V., et al., February 1990. "Experience with the first Soviet nuclear installation: irradiation doses and personnel health." Translated by Alexander Shiyakhter, Priroda, pages 1-86.

Nikipelov, Boris V., et al., May 1990. "The Kyshtym Disaster: A Close-up." Translated from the Original Title, Priroda, No. 5 (897), pages 47-75.

Nrc.gov, September 13, 2007. "Lethal Dose (LD)." U.S. Nuclear Regulatory Commission Glossary.

National Technical Information Service (NTIS), November 1991. "Final Report on DOE Nuclear Facilities." Advisory Committee on Nuclear Facility Safety, Washington, D.C., NTIS Order Number: PB92-119809.

NTIS, January 1995. "Surface Radioactivity at the Plowshare Gas-Stimulation Test Sites: Gasbuggy, Rulison, Rio Blanco." S. H. Faller, Report Number EPA/600/R-95/002.

NTIS, August 1996. "Preliminary Site Characterization Report, Rulison Site Colorado: Progress Report," Report number DOE/NV/10972-177.

NTIS, September 1996. "Assessment of hydrologic transport of radionuclides from the Gasbuggy underground nuclear test site, New Mexico," S. Earman, et al., Report Number DOE/NV/11508-16.

NTIS, December 2000. "Site Characterization Work Plan for Gasbuggy, New Mexico." Report number DOE/NV-690.

NTIS, December 2001. "Transport of gas-phase radionuclides in a fractured low-permeability reservoir." C. Cooper and J. Chapman, Report Number A-2001-03.

NTIS, January 2002. "Site Characterization Work Plan for Gnome-Coach Site, New Mexico." Report Number DOE/NV-689-Rev 1.

Radiological Assessments Corporation, August 1999. "Characterization of Releases to Surface Water from the Rocky Flats Plant." Kathryn R. Meyer with John E. Till, Ph.D. (Principal Investigator), RAC Report No. 1, Task 2: Verification and Analysis of Source Terms, - CDPHE-RFP-1, Revision 1.

Radiological Assessments Corporation, August 1999a. "Final Report – Estimated Exposure and Lifetime Cancer Incidence Risk from Plutonium Released from the 1969 Fire at the Rocky Flats Plant." Arthur S. Rood and Helen A. Grogan, with John E. Till, Ph.D. (Principal Investigator), Part of Task 3: Independent Analysis of Exposure, Dose, and Health Risk to Offsite Individuals.

Radiological Assessments Corporation, September 1999. "Technical Summary Report for the Historical Public Exposures Studies for Rocky Flats Phase II." Helen A. Grogan, Ph.D., et al., John E. Till, Ph.D. (Principal Investigator), Final Report, Part of Task 6: Technical Support for Public Involvement, RAC Report No. 14 CDPHE-RFP-1999.

Rockwell International Corporation, January 3, 1990. "An Open Letter to the People of Colorado From Rockwell International Corporation." Rocky Mountain News, page 33.

Rocky Flats Endvision, September 30, 2004. "Another empty lot on historic main street." Jackie Powers, Volume 10, Number 4, page 7.

Rocky Mountain News, November 4, 1982 "Flats vote tied to jobs, confusion," Dave Krieger, page 8

Rocky Mountain News, March 20, 1988, "DOE study cites safety risks at Rocky Flats," Janet Day, page 6.

Rocky Mountain News, June 9, 1989. "Rocky Flats search warrant to be unsealed." Sue Lindsay, page 6.

Rocky Mountain News, June 10, 1989. "FBI: Flats burned waste secretly," Sue Lindsay and Janet Day, pages 7 and 36.

Rocky Mountain News, June 11, 1989. "Waste-storage woes plague Flats." Janet Day, page 48.

Rocky Mountain News, June 15, 1989. "Flats denies N.Y. Times' reports of radioactivity." Rocky Mountain News Staff, pages 6 and 30.

Rocky Mountain News, June 15, 1989a. "No exotic chemicals found so far in Flats water," Rebecca Cantwell, page 31.

Rocky Mountain News, June 17, 1989. "Soviets admit explosion 32 years ago." Associated Press, Moscow, page 54.

Rocky Mountain News, June 18, 1989. " 'Exotic' wastes part of experiment?" Kris Newcomer, pages 14 and 20.

Rocky Mountain News, June 18, 1989a. "Neighbors suddenly feel fear." Rebecca Cantwell, pages 21 and 31.

Rocky Mountain News, June 25, 1989. "Glare of publicity has workers hot." Rebecca Cantwell, page 25.

Rocky Mountain News, May 10, 1991. "Skaggs: False data at Rocky Flats a threat." Robert Kowalski, page 3B.

Rocky Mountain News, August 20, 2004. "Rocky Flats info brouhaha." Anne Imse, page 1.

Rocky Mountain News, January 20, 2005. "Chemicals blemish Colorado's water." Debrorah Frazier, pages 4A and 8A.

Rocky Mountain News, September 2, 2006. "Flats mistrial sought," Sara Burnett, pages 4A and 12A.

Rocky Mountain News, April 21, 2007. "Lawyer fees mount in legal wrangling over Flats." Ann Imse, page 21.

Sandia National Laboratories Newsletter, April 2001. "Researching Atoms for Peace."

Sunday Camera, January 1, 1989,"State journalists vote Rocky Flats top Colorado story," Julia Rubin, page 5B

The Energy Daily, "Romer: Rocky Flats Raid was a Mistake," George Lobsenz, Wednesday, August 19, 1995, ED Volume 23, Number 155

United States Attorney, September 23, 1992. "Statement of Michael J. Norton, District of Colorado, in connection with The Rocky Flats Nuclear Weapons Plant Criminal Prosecution." U.S. Department of Justice.

United States District Court, June 6, 1989. "Search Warrant Case Number 89-730M in the Matter of the Search of The Rocky Flats Plant, United States Department of Energy, Rockwell International Corporation, Highway 93, Golden, Colorado, 80402." District of Colorado.

United States District Court, June 8, 1992. "Sentencing Hearing." District of Colorado, Criminal Action No. 92-CR-107, United States of America, Plaintiff, v. Rockwell International Corporation, Defendant, Reporter's Transcript.

United States District Court, March 26, 1992. "Defendant's Sentencing Memorandum." District of Colorado, United States of America, Plaintiff v. Rockwell International Corporation, Defendant." Brian Morgan and Lee D. Forman.

United States District Court, March 26, 1992a. "Plaintiff's Sentencing Memorandum." District of Colorado, United States of America, Plaintiff v. Rockwell International Corporation, Defendant." Michael J. Norton et al.

United States District Court, March 26, 1992b. "Plea Agreement." Michael J. Norton et al. for the U.S. Department of Justice (Plaintiff) and Lee D. Foreman et al. for Rockwell International Corporation (Defendant), District of Colorado.

United States District Court, November 10, 1997. "Defendant's Motion in Limine." District of Colorado, Rockwell International Corporation, et al., Case No. 89-N-1154.

Westword, June 21-27, 1989. "The State Knew It—And Blew It." Bryan Abas, pages 6-9.

Westword, February 3-9, 2005. "It's Toast: All the ooze that's fit to print about Rocky Flats." Patricia Calhoun, page10.

Wikipedia.org, September 8, 2007. "The SL-1, the Stationary Low-Power Reactor Number One." pages 1-6.

Wilkinson, Gregg S., et al., February 1987. "Mortality Among Plutonium And Other Radiation Workers at a Plutonium Weapons Facility." American Journal of Epidemiology, Volume 125, Number 2, pages 231-250.

Wolpe, Rep. Howard, January 4, 1993. "The Prosecution of Environmental Crimes at the Department of Energy's Rocky Flats Facility." Subcommittee on Investigations and Oversight, House Committee on Science, Space and Technology.